the
Welsh Lady from
Canaan

the Welsh Lady from Canaan

The adventures of Margaret Jones on five continents

Eirian Jones

First impression: 2012

© Copyright Eirian Jones and Y Lolfa Cyf., 2012

Cover photograph: John Thomas,
by permission of the National Library of Wales

Cover design: Y Lolfa

ISBN: 978 184771 422 0

FSC

Published and printed in Wales
on paper from well maintained forests by
Y Lolfa Cyf., Talybont, Ceredigion SY24 5HE
website www.ylolfa.com
e-mail ylolfa@ylolfa.com
tel 01970 832 304
fax 832 782

To
Rhydian and Sarah-Ann

Contents

Introduction

WHILST BROWSING THROUGH the *Cydymaith i Lenyddiaeth Cymru* [Companion to the Literature of Wales] some three years ago I came across a short note about a lady with a rather extraordinary story. Margaret Jones had been born in March 1842 in Rhosllannerchrugog, north Wales. She had published two books during her lifetime, but what intrigued me most was the fact that this Welsh lady spent time on five continents during the second half of the nineteenth century, before dying in Australia in October 1902.

In her time she was known as 'The Welsh Lady from Canaan' as she, in 1869, published a series of letters to her family from Paris, Jerusalem and Beirut in the book *Llythyrau Cymraes o Wlad Canaan* [The Letters of a Welsh Lady from Canaan]. The result of more time spent overseas was the travel book *Morocco, a'r hyn a welais yno* [Morocco, and what I saw there], which was published in 1883.

Margaret only received three weeks of schooling in Rhosllannerchrugog, which makes her experiences and accomplishments later in life all the more impressive. As a 14-year-old girl, she was employed as a maid to a family of 'returning' (or converted) Jews from Poland, in Birmingham. Her employer, the Rev. E B Frankel, worked on behalf of the London Society for the Promotion of Christianity amongst the Jews. And it was this association which turned the course of Margaret's life from being quite ordinary to something very different.

As a maid to the Frankel family, Margaret spent two years in Paris, and then four years in Jerusalem. From

1870 onwards, she travelled the length and breadth of Wales lecturing about her experiences in Canaan. Later she worked in Morocco for three years, and then travelled around the United States for two years, before emigrating to Queensland, Australia, in 1889 and marrying James Josey, a very rich man. Margaret had travelled far from the bleak coal mining village of Rhosllannerchrugog to the glory of a beautiful estate in Queensland, and it is there that she died at 60 years of age.

Whilst researching Margaret's life I came across several unexpected turns which made her story so enchanting. Her life and accomplishments would have been quite remarkable in this day and age, and I often had to remind myself that this was the story of a lady who had lived over a hundred and fifty years ago.

Some of Margaret's letters and diary extracts have been translated and extensively edited, and are included in this book.

There are very many people, on several continents, who have helped me piece together Margaret's story. I would like to give special thanks to Gwynne Williams, Bethlehem Chapel, Rhosllannerchrugog, and his cousin Eirwen for the photograph of the walking stick that Margaret sent home from Canaan. Thanks also to the kind staff of the National Library of Wales, the Union of Congregationalists and CMJ UK for their assistance, and to Dafydd Ifans for his helpful observations regarding the text. In Jerusalem, thanks to David Pileggi of Christ Church and John Arnold from the Conrad Schick Library, and to two Americans, Eric Rufa and Stacy Klodz, who were great company during my visit to Jerusalem. In Australia, thanks to the staff of John Oxley Library, State Library of Queensland, Catriona Robinson from the Ipswich Genealogical Society, Eirys Jones, Linda Josey, Lisa Kibsgaard, Bernadette Mohr, T M Palmer, Nerida Parry, Bill Parry, Debbie and Ken Downing and special thanks to Bronwen Hall, one of the descendants of Margaret's half-sister, for her help at all times. Also, thanks to Heulwen Roberts, another descendant of Margaret's family in New Zealand.

I am very indebted to Dr E Wyn James from the School of Welsh, Cardiff University, one of the very few who had already heard of Margaret Jones when I commenced my research work. His advice was priceless.

And lastly, thanks to all the staff at Y Lolfa publishers for their wonderful work and support: to Lefi Gruffudd for agreeing to publish the book, to Nia Peris for editorial guidance, to Alan Thomas for the attractive design and to Paul Williams and his hard-working team.

Strangely enough, I spend my working day in an office opposite the Congregationalist chapel in Tal-y-bont, Ceredigion, Wales. On the cold night of 17 January 1871, a lady called Margaret Jones lectured in the chapel about her experiences in Jerusalem...

Eirian Jones
April 2012

PART I

Rhosllannerchrugog, north Wales

I never beheld anything to equal some of the cottages at Rhosllanerchrugog as regards confinement, filth, and utter unfitness for human abode... The scholars were very dirty and ragged, uncouth, and not in good discipline. The noise made by them and the monitors, in proceeding with lessons, was incredible. They are a mixture of English and Welsh children; but mostly the latter, who know generally very little of the English language... The average age at which children are employed is 8... There are a great number of girls and young women employed, not in the pits but on the banks. Their employment is to carry coals on their heads to their own families.

(The Blue Books, 1847)

This is how Rhosllannerchrugog was described by commissioners of the inquiry into the state of education in Wales in 1847, in the discredited Blue Books. Margaret Jones was about to celebrate her fifth birthday when the inspectors came calling. A bleak portrait of Rhosllannerchrugog was recorded for posterity.

But to a large number of people, Rhosllannerchrugog or Rhos, as it is more widely referred to today, was a fortunate place in the middle of the nineteenth century. Fortunate, because the village sat on a lucrative seam of coal. The community, which was to become known as the 'largest village in Wales' (according to its residents anyway), attracted thousands of impoverished agricultural workers from north Wales and beyond. They were tempted by the money offered to dig for the black gold underground. Rhos may have been a dreadful place to live and work in according to the speedy eyes of the commissioners, but it was also a place which gave wages, hope and some prosperity to its inhabitants, and their families living further afield.

Today Rhos is a small town which lies around nine miles from the border with England and four miles from the town of Wrexham. Translated into English, the place name means 'moor of the heathery glade'. On a clear day, parts of seven old Welsh counties can be seen from Ponciau (or Ponkey in English), an area in the middle of the town. Llannerchrugog was the name of a local estate from the sixteenth century. The town was originally within the old parish of Ruabon, when it was referred to as Morton Above, in other words, Moor Town Above Offa's Dyke. The parish of Ruabon was divided in 1844 to form the new parishes of Ruabon, Cefn, Pen-y-cae and Rhos.

After the discovery of lucrative seams of coal in north-east Wales, Rhosllannerchrugog's fortune and future was changed forever. Once an isolated backwater, Rhos now became a large industrial village. The Holt Charter of 1563 mentions the existence of coal under Rhos, and later three pits were sunk, including Coed y Delph and Cae'r Ffynnon. The eighteenth century saw a huge expansion in the demand for coal; there was a coal mine at Ponciau as early as 1757, with a tram road linking it to the iron works at Bersham nearby, established in 1721. Before too long, many small drift mines were opened to access the coal nearer the surface. Thousands of workers moved into the area to take advantage of the prospect of some paid work. Many of these were first-language Welsh speakers from rural farming areas. Despite its proximity to the English border, Rhos became a Welsh-speaking stronghold, even though it was surrounded by English-speaking villages. This partly reflects why the village remains so Welsh, even today.

And one of those who came from the rural interior was Owen Jones, Margaret's father. He was the son of a labourer, another Owen Jones, and was born in Llandrillo-yn-Edeirnion, which lay on the borders of the counties of Merionethshire and Denbighshire. Owen, the son, was born around 1816, and like very many young men in the rural hills, he was attracted to Rhos, which was some forty miles from his place of birth, by the prospect of some work. There wasn't much hope of a better life on the hills of Merionethshire. Good land to farm was scarce. Some years had been good, but most were disappointing. There had been a famine in the Welsh countryside in 1821 during his childhood; there were more and more stomachs to be filled and there was little hope of doing that in Llandrillo. So Owen and his brother Richard headed east to Rhosllannerchrugog.

2

The village of Rhosllannerchrugog expanded rapidly at the beginning of the nineteenth century, attracting dozens of new workers to the coal mines and related industries which opened each week. As a result, housing was erected very quickly in a haphazard way all over the village with little thought to any planning. Because so many new residents came originally from the countryside, they brought the building traditions of the hills with them. For example, many houses were built as a result of a small hammer being thrown from the edge of the village, in a similar fashion to the one-night houses built in upland regions of Wales. Wherever the hammer landed would be the extent of the new household. And, although there was no need to build the houses within one night in Rhos, the houses built, nevertheless, were of very poor quality.

A gentleman called John Platt drew a map of Rhos as it was in 1835. (John Platt relied on the memory of others, as the map wasn't drawn until 1895.) This map confirms the random nature of the housing stock at that time, with the front doors of houses facing all directions.[1] Small houses would be erected next to large houses and houses were later extended on all sides to accommodate the householder's children. It was no wonder that the streets of Rhos weren't straight.

Many houses were built from Ponciau soft stone, with slate from Glynceiriog roofing the houses of the lucky ones (most roofs were thatched). There were just two rooms to each house, a room to live in and the other to sleep in. Not long after the birth of Margaret Jones, a commission was set up by the government to report on the standard of education in Wales. They not only looked at educational matters, but also at living conditions in Rhos around 1846–7. These are the remarks of John James, one of the assistants of Henry Vaughan Johnson, who travelled through north Wales making notes for the Blue Books:

> I then visited many cottages in different parts of the village.
> Some of these consist of a single room from 9 to 12 feet square;
> others have in addition a sort of a lean-to, forming a separate
> place to sleep in. They are in general void of furniture; but in
> some I found a bed which is made to accommodate double
> numbers by arranging the occupants feet to feet. The roofs are
> wattled; sometimes plastered over with mortar, sometimes bare;
> others are of straw, and full of large holes open to the sky, which
> are frequently the only means of admitting light. Each of these
> hovels contains on average a family of six children, with their
> parents. If they comprise two rooms the parents sleep in one,
> and the children in the other; if there is but one room, all sleep
> together.[2]

John James recalls visiting a row of cottages in Rhos on 20 January 1847:

I went in company with the Rev. P M Richards, the officiating minister of the district to visit some of the houses of the colliers at Rhosllanerchrugog; and though I have seen St Giles's, Cow Cross, Wapping, and other places in the metropolis where the houses of the poor are unfit to live in, I never beheld anything to equal some of the cottages at Rhosllanerchrugog as regards confinement, filth, and utter unfitness for human abode. Cottage, No. 1, consists of one low room, about 12 feet square, containing an old man perfectly black with dirt, lying on a bed of rags and filth. In the same cottage lives his son, who is in consumption. No. 2 consists of one small room, dirty and so close, that the atmosphere was insupportable. The floor was alternately of mud and stone. In the centre an idiot was seated on a stool. Her mother, an old woman, 70 or 80 years of age was lying on a filthy bed beside her, reduced to a skeleton with disease. The room was without an article of what would be called furniture. No. 3 contains only one room, in which live a man and his two idiot children, both about 20 years old. No. 4, a cottage of one room, contains a father and mother, their daughter and her husband, occupying two beds placed close together, the room being very small. The beds are filthy, the furniture miserable, and the ventilation bad. No. 5, a cottage of one room, inhabited by two adult sisters and their two adult brothers. All occupy the same bed, which may be enlarged a little, but is still the same bed. The room is low-roofed and ill-ventilated. None of these houses had a necessary anywhere near them, nor did I see such a thing in the whole village.[3]

The reports noted that most homes in Rhos could be described thus, and one reason given for this was the fact that the poor tenants had to pay a ground rent of between seven and fifteen shillings per annum as well as a rent to the landlord. And as they lived in low-quality housing, the inhabitants were prone to suffer oftener from ill health. However, the reports did give the odd example of a household which was 'unusually neat and clean... containing a father and a mother well and neatly dressed, a son 18 years old, and a daughter aged 20. All these sleep together in the same room, which is about 9 or 10 feet square.'[4]

Margaret Jones was born in a house such as this in March 1842. Soon, she would have a brother, John, born a year later. But becoming pregnant frequently and the inferior living conditions took their toll on the health of her mother, Ann, who died shortly after the birth of another baby in April 1847, at the age of 28 years. Owen Jones would marry three times and see his three wives predecease him. He would father ten children, with very many of them not surviving to adulthood.

3

The reaction to the Blue Books amidst communities such as Rhosllannerchrugog was as severe as the criticisms laid out in the reports. The generally held belief was that the reports portrayed Welsh-speaking communities inaccurately and unfavourably. After all, the main purpose of the reports was to convince the government that the teaching of lessons through the Welsh language in schools was lowering the standard of education received by the Welsh. There is little doubt that the housing stock was of poor quality at that time, but to read the reports, one felt that whole communities were also being portrayed as being severely disadvantaged.

Most men in Rhos, like Owen Jones, and later his sons John and Thomas, worked in the coal mines. Life was particularly hard for them, with little recompense for spending a twelve-hour shift underground in dangerous and dirty conditions. The Blue Books also describe the difficulties of this arduous life:

> The children are employed in these mines at a very early age, some to carry food to their parents, others to clear the banks, and many work in the mines. The mines and quarries are for coal, lime, iron &c. The children are employed in the mines and pits to open the doors for ventilating the pits, to drive horses which are employed below, and to drag small carts on their hands and knees.

The average age at which children are employed is 8... There
are a great number of girls and young women employed, not in
the pits but on the banks. Their employment is to carry coals on
their heads to their own families, to remove obstructions from
the mouths of the pits, to wind up materials from the bottom by
the wheels, and in many cases to load coals. They acquire a taste
for this employment at an early age, and will often leave good
situations in respectable families, when they are grown to be
young women, in order to return to their old occupation.[5]

The local vicar, the Rev. P M Richards, had more to add to
the reports about the young women of the area, concluding
that 'throughout the district the women have no kind of
knowledge of the duties of their sex, or of common household
occupations and requirements; that till lately needlework
was unknown among them'.[6]

It seemed that so many women were employed in mining
that it had a strong immoral effect on them. The authors
were of the opinion that it was degrading for women to do
this work, mainly because of the kind of people they were
working with. As a result, young girls were becoming 'bold
and impudent, and wantonly vicious, sing[ing] the vilest
songs, and publicly behav[ing] in the most indecent manner
whilst engaged in this occupation'.[7]

It is quite obvious that only the most startling examples
were included in the reports. There is no record of any
female member of Margaret Jones's family having to
endure the indignity of working down the mines. On the
marriage certificate of Ann Phillips, Margaret's mother, her
occupation is stated as being a servant before marriage.
Indeed, Margaret herself would be sent away to work as a
maid in the Llangollen area at the age of fourteen.

Perhaps gossip and hearsay were the main sources for
much of what was recorded in the Blue Books. The respectful
congregations of the many chapels in Rhos were infuriated
to read that personal morals were very low in the village.
The origin of many of these accusations was the local vicar,

the Rev. P M Richards. The Nonconformist chapels were thriving at that time in Rhos, and the vicar was envious of their success. Indeed, the reports not only placed the blame for the poverty, poor housing and lack of prospects for the locals on the Welsh language, but also on the ideas and beliefs of the Nonconformists for worsening the situation.

However the Blue Books weren't the only source to show how difficult life was in Rhos in the middle of the nineteenth century. A Baptist minister, the Rev. Ellis Evans, sent a letter to his brother in the United States in 1831, summarising his thoughts about living conditions in the area. He told his brother of the difficulty in securing work, the poor wages of those in employment – goods in the shops were expensive, and there were many people starving. When colliers had gathered together to plead for a rise in their wages from 2/6 to 3/– a day, troopers had been called to disperse them. One of the mine owners had been heard to say that he would rather see his men eat grass before he'd give them a wage rise.[8]

Coal mining was physically hard work for both sexes, and was even harder still when the quality of the food was inadequate. Only plain food, with little choice, made it to the plates of the lucky few – food such as barley bread and milky-potatoes mostly, with cheese and some pork for special occasions. Perhaps there would be treacle instead of sugar, but very little butter and milk was available regularly.[9] What made matters worse for the inhabitants of Rhos was that many of these foodstuffs on sale there were much more expensive than in neighbouring Wrexham. As the Blue Books say:

> The truck system goes on at Rhosllanerchrugog or the
> neighbourhood. If it is not carried on directly, it is indirectly.
> A very small portion of the wages due to the operatives is paid
> in money. They receive tickets, which they must take to the
> shop. If this method of payment is not compulsory upon the
> workmen, it amounts to the same thing, for they would not be

employed if they declined to receive tickets instead of money. The price of these provisions in these shops is much higher than in Wrexham. 10d. is paid for bacon instead of 8d., and 4 lbs of flour are sold for 1s., when 6 lbs are sold for the same price within a distance of 5 miles. The magistrates have offered to put down the practice, but the workmen will not come forward with evidence, knowing that if they were to do so, they would lose their employment.[10]

This piece of evidence came from Thomas Francis, a Calvinistic Methodist minister and shopkeeper in Wrexham.

One of the reasons why many families enclosed a piece land with their house in Rhos was in order to be able to rear an animal such as a pig or cow. Many families kept two pigs, one to feed the family and the other was fattened for sale to buy other goods. If space allowed on the homestead, potatoes would be planted and some chickens kept.

Clothing in the mid nineteenth century was very simple. When a collier was able to buy a new woollen jacket and cloth breeches, he would wear them a number of times to chapel before wearing them to go down the mine. If money allowed, some would try to keep clothes for Sunday best: a frock coat, fancy waistcoat, coloured cloth breeches and a silk hat. Women would wear a long dress with long sleeves and an underskirt, with a small bonnet. They would wear a long cloak in the winter months.

One of Thomas Charles's peripatetic schools was established in Rhos as early as 1789. Later, the private Boncddu School opened its doors in 1804. Around 1840, a lady called Mrs Roberts ran Laurel House School for around forty boys and girls, who paid sixpence a week to learn a curriculum which primarily concentrated on sewing.[11] The reports' inspectors didn't visit any of these schools. But, the Blue Books do mention two schools which were opened in the 1840s and one of the assistants to the inspector, John James, visited both. The first was the National School which was established in 1844 with aid from the education committee

of the National Society. John James visited this school on
19 January 1847:

> Rhosllanerchrugog National School, – A school for boys and girls,
> taught separately by a master and a mistress, in a school built for
> the purpose. Number of boys, 57; girls, 66; monitors, 13. Subjects
> taught – reading, writing, and arithmetic; the Scriptures and the
> Church Catechism. Fees 1d. per week, and 6d. entrance. Income
> of teacher, £29. Of the 94 scholars who were present, 69 had been
> members for more than one year. I found only 14 who could read
> with ease, while 17 were ignorant of the alphabet. Among 27 copy-
> books, only one contained good writing; and of 13 boys learning
> arithmetic, no one was proficient even in the compound rules; 7
> could solve a few easy questions of mental arithmetic. The girls
> do not learn arithmetic. This deficiency in secular knowledge
> is partly owing to the time and attention devoted to religious
> education. Besides the Scripture and the Church Catechism, the
> children learn prayers, 'Faith and Duty', sacred music, and the
> 'Holy Seasons and Festivals of the Church'. The minister of the
> district assists the teachers in imparting religious instruction. I
> found 12 children who could answer questions upon Scripture, 8
> of them in the Catechism, among 34 examined, and only 2 could
> repeat answers correctly. Only 8 children possessed any available
> knowledge of the English language. The master is 25 years of
> age. He has not been trained at a normal school, but spent seven
> months in 1844, at two National schools to learn the system. He
> understands English well, but sometimes speaks ungrammatically.
> He seldom interprets; he appears to have had little education.
> His control over the school is defective; while I was examining
> one class, the rest of the children and their monitors were either
> playing or staring at me. The mistress is a married woman. She
> had an infant in arms with her in the school. She has never been
> trained at all, and has received very little education. She speaks
> English very incorrectly. She teaches needlework daily.[12]

The reports sum up that:

> Divine service is performed in the school-room on Sunday, until
> sufficient funds can be obtained for the erection of a church.
> There is a house for the schoolmaster, which is at present

occupied by the officiating minister of the district, who pays a rent to the master. With the exception of the children's pence, it appears that nothing is obtained from the locality for the support of the school, which is indebted to the officiating minister to the amount of £30. This assistance cannot be continued, and it does not appear how the school will in future be enabled to continue in operation.[13]

A British and Foreign School was established in December 1846 by the 'dissenters of Rhosllanerchrugog' as the reports described them. Margaret and her brother John attended this school for a short time. The school was run by a committee of 13 people selected from the different denominations of the Nonconformists. The schoolmaster was offered a salary of £50, but at the time of John James's visit only six pounds had been collected for the salary. These are John James's remarks:

Rhosllanerchrugog British School, – A school for boys and girls, taught together by a master in a Calvinistic Methodist Chapel. Number of boys, 180; of girls, 87; number employed as monitors, 9. Subjects professed to be taught – the Scriptures, reading, writing, arithmetic, and the History of England. Fees, 1d. and 2d. per week. Master's salary, £50. I visited the school... when it had been only six weeks in operation. I found 192 scholars present; only 10 could write with ease, and 91 ignorant of the alphabet. Only 3 could answer easy questions upon Scripture correctly; 38 were learning to write upon slates, but few of these could draw a tolerably straight line. There were only 17 copies, none of which contained good writing. A class of 11 had commenced arithmetic, but none understood Compound Multiplication. In history, there were 2 only who had committed to memory a few facts with reference to the early history of England. The scholars were very dirty and ragged, uncouth, and not in good discipline. The noise made by them and the monitors, in proceeding with lessons, was incredible. They are a mixture of English and Welsh children; but mostly the latter, who know generally very little of the English language. The master is only 21 years of age. He was trained at the Borough-road National School for six months. His questions upon the subjects of the lessons were poor, and slowly conceived.

He is necessarily inexperienced, and it is difficult to imagine a school where more experience is required. Though he appears anxious to do his best, he does not and cannot control the school, which is not only numerous, but consists of children who, being altogether uncivilized, appear to require discipline even more than instruction. It is impossible, in a school so recently established, to have monitors competent to teach; nine monitors are employed in this school, all of whom were found to be incompetent. Upon these monitors, and the master, aged 21, depends the education of 267 children. The chapel is large, but insufficiently warmed and very inconvenient for the purposes of a British school. It was very dirty. The school apparatus, which were provided by the Committee, are all insufficient. For this school of 267 scholars of both sexes, there is no outbuilding of any kind; 71 pupils are above 10 years of age. It does not appear that there is any instruction in needlework in this school.[14]

Harsh words indeed for a school which, as quoted, had only been opened six weeks previously. One wonders what John James would have had to say if he knew that this school was held at Jerusalem (the Calvinistic Methodist chapel) on Brook Street for one month, and then transferred to Bethlehem (the Congregational chapel), Hall Street, the next month? One of the pupils' tasks was to carry benches from one chapel to the other (a distance of half a mile). And this went on for another twenty years, until a purpose-built school opened on 6 June 1865.[15]

4

The Anglican Church and the Nonconformists had established schools in Rhos within a few years of one another. Rhosllannerchrugog parish was created in 1844 and the Church of St John the Evangelist was consecrated in October 1853. It offered services in both Welsh and English, and this Romanesque Revival church in a Norman style would become a grade II listed building. The church closed in 2004.

This one church was outnumbered by chapels in Rhos. Historically, Rhos has been renowned for the number of religious buildings per head of the population. Although most have now closed their doors, there are 35 religious buildings within one square mile in the middle of Rhos today, with the vast majority of them being Nonconformist chapels. The Calvinist Methodists began their cause in Rhos in 1765. Their present chapel, Jerusalem, in Brook Street was built in 1837. It has a seating capacity of around 1,200 and is one of the largest chapels in north Wales. In 1851, it was not unusual to see 700 people attending evening service, even during inclement weather. The average attendance at a service in Jerusalem was around 900 members.

The Baptists' cause commenced in Pearson Street in 1793. Stone was carried by horse and cart from a quarry in Ponkey Park, with the ladies carrying stone not only in their aprons but on their heads too.

Margaret Jones and her family were members with the Congregationalists. The Congregational Church believed that each church should be accountable for its own governance, without any interference from the civil state or an external church authority. Amongst prominent Congregationalists were Williams of Wern (who was very well known to Rhos Congregationalists), William Rees, 'Gwilym Hiraethog' (a keen supporter of Margaret Jones's literary aspirations) and Michael D Jones (who led the movement to establish a Welsh colony, or *Gwladfa*, in Patagonia).

The first Congregational chapel was established in Rhos in 1810, in the home of collier Ishmael Jones (1794–1876) at Plas-yn-Pant, Ponciau. Their first minister was one of the most famous preachers in Wales, Williams of Wern. William Williams (1781–1840) was one of the three touring preachers most revered during their lifetimes in Wales (the other two being John Elias (1774–1841) with the Calvinistic Methodists and Christmas Evans (1766–1838) with the Baptists). Williams was born in Llanfachreth, Merionethshire and, after hearing a remarkable man called Rhys Davies (1772–1847) preach when he was thirteen years old, Williams joined the Congregational Church. After attending the Academy in Wrexham, he was ordained at Wern in 1808.[16] He travelled from place to place on horseback, preaching to large gatherings. He was an entrancing and eloquent preacher. Williams saw potential as a preacher in one of his congregation, the collier Ishmael Jones. He encouraged him to attend Hackney Academy, and after being ordained Ishmael Jones travelled the country as a preacher, before returning to live in his native Rhos in 1847.

Williams of Wern oversaw the building of Bethlehem, the Congregational chapel in Hall Street in 1812. It was built on the site of four chamber houses and four pigsties. Much like Jerusalem, the chapel was built by the colliers and clay workers to no formal plan and without any official permission either. In 1843 the chapel was extended, and a gallery built to accommodate a congregation of up to 1,200 people. By now the chapel measured 54 yards by 45 yards and the cost of the extension amounted to £950 for the members. The Congregationalists' returns note that this chapel had 36 unoccupied seats, 390 other seats with room for a further 350 to stand on their feet. The records of 30 March 1851 show that 383 were present for the service in the morning with 550 attending evening service, despite it being a stormy night.[17] Normally, the average attendance would be 650, with 380 attending Sunday school in Margaret Jones's day. An organ was installed in Bethlehem in 1862 when the chapel was extended once again, and £1,800 was spent on another extension in 1889, adding 200 more seats to the chapel. Later, Bethlehem Chapel would be renowned for its *Rundbogenstil* (round, arched) front and a gallery which was situated underneath the organ and behind the pulpit.

Jerusalem had its own familiar name, Capel Mawr (big chapel), and so too did Bethlehem, which was known as Capel Bychan (small chapel). There are many reasons as to how it got this unofficial name. One reason may be the fact that the original chapel measured only ten yards by thirteen yards before several extensions. But perhaps another reason comes from a sinister story from the nineteenth century. A baby with two heads was born near the chapel, which was located in an area described as the 'slum' of Rhosllannerchrugog at the time. As many of the villagers were highly superstitious, they did not want to see the baby (which did not survive) buried in the village cemetery, so, the little one (*bychan*) was buried inside Bethlehem Chapel. In 1926, the interior of the chapel was refurbished and redecorated and the remains of the baby were discovered. It was decided to leave it in its original burial place, which is, apparently, under the third pew.

Another possible reason for calling the chapel Capel Bychan comes from the pseudonym of one of Bethlehem's ministers. Robert Thomas (1809–80) was a poet, and was known in literary circles as Ap Vychan. He was raised in Llanuwchllyn, Merionethshire and learnt the rules of strict metre poetry (*cynganeddion*) from his father. He was apprenticed as a blacksmith, and travelled the countryside following that occupation. By 1835 he had been ordained as a minister with the Congregationalists. In time, he became a Professor of Divinity at the Independent College in Bala where Michael D Jones was principal.

He was the minister at Bethlehem between 1848 and 1855, and therefore knew Margaret's family well. Indeed, Margaret mentions his greatest poetic feat in a letter from Jerusalem to her parents in 1866. Ap Vychan won the chair for an ode at the Chester National Eisteddfod in that year. His chair had been made out of oak obtained from the roof of the famous interlude writer Twm o'r Nant's home (Thomas Edwards; 1739–1810). There is little doubt that

Ap Vychan's interest in literature and poetry inspired his congregation at Bethlehem too.

Singing was very important at Bethlehem and, from time to time, its singing festivals would attract noted conductors such as Dr Joseph Parry (1841–1903), the composer of the hymn tune 'Aberystwyth' and the first Professor of Music at University College of Wales, Aberystwyth. One reason for such renown for Bethlehem's singing was the fact that a superb organ had been installed in the chapel. At one time, Bethlehem's organist was a local-born man, Dr Caradog Roberts (1878–1935). Having been apprenticed as a carpenter, he went on to study music at Oxford University.[18] Later, he became Director of Music at the University College of North Wales, Bangor. He edited many Congregational Church hymn books and was also the composer of a number of famous Welsh hymn tunes, including 'Rachie'.

Bethlehem's popular Sunday school was established in 1843. The Blue Books note the following statistics for January 1847, when Margaret could have been present: there were 37 males and 38 females under the age of fifteen, with 61 males and 60 females over the age of fifteen registered as members. When the inspectors visited there were 82 males and 68 females present. They were taught by 17 male teachers and three female teachers. It was noted that 131 were able to read the Scriptures and that only 30 were allowed to attend day school.

The chapels were the main centres of religion, culture and entertainment in Rhosllannerchrugog. There was a public house for each chapel as well, with the tavern, Sun and Dragon, only a few doors away from Bethlehem Chapel. Rhos was a lively place to grow up in during the 1840s and 1850s despite the severe hardships, the shoddily-built dwellings, the lack of nutritious food for long periods throughout the year, and the exploitation of a workforce who never knew if they would return to their families safely at the end of their shifts each day. Death was a frequent visitor above ground as well as below. But one senses that there was a close and happy community on the whole in Rhos. The chapels thronged, with hundreds attending services. The people feared God and knew how to do right by one another. Life in Rhos was hard, and a struggle to survive, but it was also a place where characters were built and ambitions fired.

5

One such character, with a good deal of ambition, was Margaret Jones, the eldest daughter of Owen Jones. Her mother, Ann Phillips, came from Rhos. She had been born in 1818, the third child of miner John Phillips and his wife Sarah. Owen and Ann were married at the parish church in Wrexham on 27 July 1839 by curate Edward Edwards. Both were residents of the township of Esclusham Below. The marriage certificate seems to suggest that Owen could write his name, but Ann could not (so too incidentally their witnesses, Richard, Owen's brother, and Sarah, Ann's sister).

The couple settled into their home in Hall Street, on the same road as Bethlehem Chapel. It is thought that Margaret was born in March 1842.[19] She was their first child to survive. A year later, Margaret had a brother, John. Perhaps Ann became pregnant again several times after 1843. She was with child in April 1847, and gave birth on 12 April. Ann died the following day of 'Puerperal Convulsions 26 Hours Certified', as a result of the birth. It appears that the little baby died too.

Owen Jones was a widower, a miner, with two small children to raise as well. It is not surprising therefore that he soon remarried. In the spring of 1849, he married Catherine who came from Llangar, Meirionethshire. Their son, Thomas, was born in 1850.

Owen Jones's little family grew up in Hall Street, Rhosllannerchrugog. They worshipped regularly at Bethlehem Chapel, and Margaret and John and Thomas would go to school from time to time. The family would pray fervently that their father returned home unharmed from the pit each night.

PART II

From
Bethlehem to Jerusalem

*It is written in the Talmud (Kiddushim 49B) that God divided
Beauty into ten parts, allocating nine parts to Jerusalem and
one part to the rest of the world. He then separated Science
into ten parts, and again gave nine parts to Jerusalem. Then
finally, however, He divided Sorrow into ten parts, assigning in
the same manner nine parts to Jerusalem and one part to the
rest of the world. No other parable so aptly captures both the
dramatic mystery and bitter allure of the city of Jerusalem...*

(Roberto Copello, *Jerusalem*, p.9)

An obituary written soon after Margaret's death in 1902
notes that she only received a total of three weeks schooling
in Rhosllannerchrugog. As soon as children were mature
enough to be trusted with paid work, they were encouraged
to leave the home and seek a living.

That was Margaret's destiny too. Around 1856, when
she was about fourteen years old, she left the family home
to go to live in Llangollen, not too distant a location from
Rhos, but miles away from the greyness and dust of the
coal mines. As a fourteen year-old, her brother John went to
work in the coal mines (and according to the 1861 census,
he was lucky enough to get work as a mine clerk).

William Wright, a shopkeeper and farmer, and his
wife Mary became Margaret's new employer and family.

They lived in quite a substantial house called Garth, and employed Margaret as a maid. According to the 1861 census, there weren't any children in the household, yet it was large enough a house to justify keeping two maids, Margaret and Mary Ann Jones.

The beautiful town of Llangollen, today the site of an annual international eisteddfod, lay on the banks of the river Dee. The bridge which crosses the river, built around 1500, is regarded as one of the seven wonders of Wales. The Llangollen canal, which opened in 1808, was designed by Thomas Telford as a means of carrying goods to England. On the outskirts of the town lay Plas Newydd, the home of Eleanor Butler and Sarah Ponsonby, known as 'The Ladies of Llangollen'. The poets Byron, Shelley and Wordsworth were frequent visitors to Plas Newydd.

William Wright was born in Denbighshire around 1813. His wife Mary came from Llansanffraid, Conwy and she was born in 1811. It is hard to overestimate the influence that being a part of this family had on Margaret's future. Margaret's life expectations can't have been very high – perhaps to work as a maid, and then marry and have a family and keep a house. But an event, many miles away in Birmingham, shattered those expectations and gave Margaret incredible opportunities, and changed the course of her life for ever.

A member of William Wright's family was about to marry. Perhaps Margaret Wright was William's sister, or maybe a cousin. The 37 year-old had recently become betrothed to a widower, the Rev. Elias Benjamin Frankel. He had three small daughters, and they needed to be looked after. And it was then that Margaret's name arose in a conversation between William and Margaret Wright. Surely his maid would be perfect to look after the daughters of the minister? Margaret Jones was a religious girl, yet full of life. In no time, Margaret Jones had packed her belongings and was on her way to the Lozells area of Birmingham.

The city of Birmingham was some one hundred miles from Rhosllannerchrugog, a comparatively short distance compared to how far Margaret travelled throughout the rest of her life. Elias Benjamin Frankel, the Polish head of the household was an Ashkenazim Jew originally.[1] He had been converted or proselytized to the Christian faith in Poland and became a 'returned' Christian. [2] He worked as the curate of St Silas Church in Lozells and would later become a missionary on behalf of the London Society for the Promotion of Christianity amongst the Jews. Margaret, most probably, had never heard of this society, but she knew that his work was of a Christian nature and that was enough to assure her that the arrangements for her future would work.

When Elias Frankel decided to 'return' to Christianity in Poland in 1847, he left his home and family: father Simon, who was a merchant, his mother, five brothers and two sisters. He risked alienating his family for the rest of his life and he probably knew that he would never see them again.[3]

By 1850, the 23-year-old Elias had become a British subject and had married Elizabeth Myers. Elizabeth had been born around 1827 in Stanhope, County Durham. They were married at Christ Church, Southwark, London, in 1850, shortly before the couple left for Lyon in eastern France. Their first daughter, Maria Louisa, was born there in 1852, with another daughter, Emilie, born in 1854. The Frankels returned to England before their last daughter, Elizabeth Hannah, was born in Birmingham in 1859.

On his return to England, Elias Frankel became the church curate of St Silas in Lozells, Birmingham. After a few happy years in the city, tragedy struck in 1861 when Elizabeth Frankel died of pulmonary tuberculosis at the age of 34 years. Elias had three grief-stricken daughters who had suddenly lost their mother. He was keen to remarry and did so sixteen months later, in October 1862. Margaret Wright became his wife at a church in Lambeth, London, and

Margaret Jones became a maid and nurse to the three girls.

The newlyweds returned to Birmingham after their wedding. Margaret Jones had by now established herself within the family, and was good company for the children and experienced enough to run the household properly. But the house in Lozells brought back painful memories to Elias Frankel. And anyway, he wanted to have a fresh start with his new wife. It's no surprise, therefore, that he accepted an invitation from the London Society for the Promotion of Christianity amongst the Jews to go to Paris as a missionary on their behalf, less than two months after his marriage to Margaret Wright. The family started their journey to Paris on 4 December 1862.[4]

A year earlier, Margaret had been a maid about to celebrate her twentieth birthday, enjoying life with friends in the beautiful town of Llangollen and travelling home to Rhos when the opportunity arose, to visit family and attend Bethlehem Chapel. In the meantime, she had experienced an incredible change in her life already, living in a noisy, industrial city, and now she was on her way to live in a cosmopolitan city on the European mainland, where she wouldn't hear a word of Welsh spoken. One wonders if she was given the choice to return home to Wales rather than follow the family to Paris? Perhaps she felt sorry for the girls. They had also seen tremendous change in the past eighteen months; if Margaret left them, they would have to endure even more changes. But Margaret was a brave girl, as well as being adventurous, and she showed these attributes for the first time in 1862, character traits which would sustain her and form a pattern to her life for the next forty years.

2

Elias Frankel worked for a London-based missionary society. This society worked mainly with the Jews. It's unlikely that Margaret would have come across any Jews before joining the Frankel family, nor would she have been aware of the work of the London Society for the Promotion of Christianity amongst the Jews. But Margaret and her fellow worshippers at Bethlehem would have known of the work of Welsh Nonconformist missionaries in overseas territories. Some of the most prominent missionaries of the nineteenth century were raised in the Nonconformist chapels of Wales and their work in these faraway places still resonates to this day.

Missionaries from Wales were amongst the first to be recruited by the London Missionary Society, a non-denominational society which was established in 1795 and sent hundreds of missionaries around the world. Thomas Charles (1755–1814) from Bala, who persuaded the SPCK to publish Welsh-language Bibles in 1799 and was one of the founders of the Bible Society in 1804, was one of the London Missionary Society's staunchest supporters. John Davies (1772–1855), an associate of the Welsh hymnist Ann Griffiths, was the first Welsh missionary for the London Missionary Society when he was sent to Tahiti in 1800. A little later, the Congregational Church started sending missionaries overseas, predominantly to the South Sea Islands, India, China and Madagascar.

Two Welshmen had great influence in China. Griffith John (1831–1912) travelled to Hankow in 1855, and spent more than five decades travelling the country, preaching the gospel, establishing churches, schools, a theological college and also a home for leprosy sufferers.[5] Timothy Richard (1845–1919) from Ffaldybrenin was sent by the Baptist Missionary Society to Chafoo, Shantung and then Shanghai in China. He was known throughout the country as 'Li T'i-mo-tai' and was an academic, teacher, author, philanthropist, missionary, statesman, mandarin and counsellor to the courts. It is thought that he more or less governed China for a while. Amongst the Welsh, only David Lloyd George (1863–1945), United Kingdom Prime

Minister (1916–22), has exercised more governmental power.[6]

The Casia Hills of north-east India were the final destination for many Calvinist Methodist missionaries in the nineteenth century. Welsh missionaries were sent to Africa too: the Wesleyan missionary William Davies (1785–1851) was one of the first to arrive in Sierra Leone and Thomas Lewis (1859–1929) spread the Baptist message in the Congo and Cameroon.[7]

Missionaries were followed by their wives and children and, later, by doctors and teachers. A thriving missionary base would have schools, a hospital, accommodation for the missionaries and their families and those who had been proselytized to Christianity, and perhaps a printing press, as well as a church.[8] But this work was costly, and the sums needed to build and maintain missionary bases were great.

As a result, large amounts of money were needed and that is why the pages of Welsh denominational journals of the day, such as the Congregationalist's *Dysgedydd* [The Instructor] and the Calvinist Methodist's *Y Drysorfa* [The Treasury], were filled with stories, reports and letters from places across the world that one would be hard-pressed to find on a map. In turn, this 'glamorous' work that these Welshmen and women undertook overseas resulted in large amounts of money being raised in Wales to help with the missions, provided by the not so brave congregations back home. The Welsh admired their missionaries a great deal and they were regarded with awe in their day. Their 'successes' in foreign fields did wonders to raise Welsh self-esteem, especially after the publication of the discredited Blue Books.[9]

The missionary societies varied in the way in which they worked in the field, but the main objective of each society was to give a Bible to everyone. But the London Society for the Promotion of Christianity amongst the Jews differed from this notion. Their main aim was to share the New

Testament amongst the Jews and bring the teachings of
Jesus Christ into their lives.

3

The London Society for the Promotion of Christianity
amongst the Jews was Elias Frankel's employers for nearly
twenty years,[10] and missionaries from this society were
instrumental in persuading the young Frankel in Poland to
'return' to the Christian faith. The London Jews Society (that
is, The London Society for the Promotion of Christianity
amongst the Jews/LJS) was established in 1808. Their simple
objective was to proselytize Jews from all parts of society to
become Christians.

The idea of the Jews, God's elected people, accepting
Jesus Christ as his Son was not new at the beginning of the
nineteenth century. Efforts had been made to compel the
Jews for centuries, but early endeavours were not orderly.
Between the sixth century and the Protestant Revival there
hadn't been many attempts at all to evangelise the Jews.
The New Testament was not translated into Hebrew until
the fifteenth century, and, in truth, the Jews were more
likely to be treated with contempt than to be evangelized
by the Christians.

Jews began to arrive in England in large numbers
during the reign of King William I (1066–87), when they
purchased the right to come to live there. They settled
together in places such as London, Oxford and Stamford.
The Jews had multiplied to such an extent by the reign
of Henry I (1100–35) that the Jews started to proselytize
the Christians. As a result, monks were sent to towns to
counteract the ideas of the Jews. Jews were falsely accused
of robbery, pillage and massacre. By 1290, all the Jews in
England were sent into exile.

As the centuries went by and the effect of the Revival

reduced prejudicial feeling, some Jews began to make their homes in Britain once more. By 1657, a piece of land was given over in Stepney, London, for a synagogue. But although life improved for some Jews in England, the majority were still treated like strangers.

Opportunities improved for the Jews with the dawn of the Victorian age; by now Jews were even eligible to stand as Members of Parliament. Thousands of Jews came to settle in Britain from all over the globe. Areas such as Spitalfields and Whitechapel in London were very nearly completely Jewish, and were known as 'Palestine in London'. And the émigrés brought a jargon language with them, called Yiddish: a mixture of German, Hebrew, Polish and English.[11]

4

The history of the formation of the LJS stems from about 1801 when a Christian Jew, Joseph Frey, came to England from Berlin to work for the London Missionary Society. The work of this society amongst the Jews (they also worked overseas, as noted earlier), was to establish schools for Jewish boys and girls and preach sermons to them. But Frey wanted to do more for the Jews, but the London Missionary Society was reluctant to give him the resources to do so. Frey decided to establish his own missionary society, and on 4 August 1808, in a chapel in the East End of London, 'a small and unpretending association, consisting of a few influential men, was formed under the title of "The London Society for the purpose of visiting and relieving the sick and distressed, and instructing the ignorant, especially such as are of the Jewish nation", with Mr Frey as its President.'[12]

As work started amongst the Jews, members of all Christian denominations worked for the LJS. The Duke of Kent was elected patron of the society. In the early years the LJS concentrated on improving the living conditions of the Jews. Then, a 'Jews Chapel' was established in Spitalfields and sermons and lectures were given to curious Jews by ministers from the all denominations. A school was established also, and by 1812 there were 83 Jewish boys and girls attending. In the same year, 41 adult Jews were baptised into the church of Christ, the largest number since the days of the Apostles.

The Jews were very poor, and the LJS employed special measures to try to encourage the Jews to listen to their message. For example, Jews would receive free clothing and food provided they attended meetings and showed interest in the church of Christ. Manufacturing units were established to teach and train the Jews in the fields of printing and making cloth, for example.[13] Just about anything was tried to attract the Jews into Christ's fold, whilst also trying to prove to the many detractors who ridiculed the society, that they were trying to achieve much more than converting the Jews.

At this time, the society had many opponents and they were very vocal, with some arguing that the money allocated to converting Jews to Christianity would have been better spent returning lost Protestant sheep into the fold. Many complained that the LJS treated the Jews as 'slow' people. But, according to many members of the society, if the Jews were treated firmly, like problem children, then some good might come of them in the end. The pain inflicted on the Jews was unfortunate, but totally necessary, in the opinion of many members of the society.

In 1814 the society's new headquarters, Palestine Place, was opened in Bethnal Green, London. The church there was the first place of worship in Britain for Christian Jews. It would become the centre of the LJS's missionary work for the next eighty years.[14] Branches of the society were established across Britain and Ireland, from Weymouth to Glasgow and from Dublin to Norwich. And as the society grew, so too did the differences between the denominations who ran the society. For example, Nonconformist members of the society were unable to officiate the sacrament in the Palestine Place church because it had been consecrated as an Anglican church. By 1815, the LJS had become an exclusively Anglican society.

5

A New Testament in the Hebrew language was published in 1817. It had a limited circulation in Britain, but was very popular amongst the Jews in continental Europe. In 1817–18 a member of the society, Lewis Way, went on a tour of Holland, Germany and Russia, distributing copies of the Hebrew New Testament on his journey. He received a warm welcome, and Way came to the conclusion that the Jewish population of Russian Poland were ripe for evangelizing. In July 1818, a branch of the society was established in Poland. In order to continue the work on the continent, an education facility was established to train foreign missionaries in 1821. By the 1830s there was a dramatic expansion in the work of the society, not only on the European continent but also in the Levant and India.

In 1795, when Poland had been carved up between Russia, Prussia and Austria, it was estimated that five million Jews lived in the country. In an area of the country known as the 'Pale of Jewish Settlement', the Jewish population was rising by some 80,000 per annum. Poland had been the home of Jewish people for centuries and, as a result, orthodox and conservative Judaism was very strong.

The LJS commenced work in Poland in 1821. The task of the missionaries was very difficult at first, and one of the reasons for this was the colloquial languages of the 'Pale': a mixture of Judeao-Polish, Jüdisch-Deutsch, and Jüdisch or Yiddish. The people were simply unable to understand the Hebrew New Testament because they did not use Hebrew words.

The pioneers of the work in Poland were local men: the Rev. B N Solomon, the Rev. J F Nitschke, a Hebrew Christian and J C Moritz. Solomon translated the New Testament to the local colloquial languages, and the three travelled the land preaching and distributing the New Testament. Warsaw became the centre of the mission, before other branches were established in Posen and Krakow. The work of the society flourished for decades: in 1825 the baptism of a Jewess attracted an audience of nearly 200 Jews.[15] And of course, amongst those attracted was Elias Frankel. Elias had been born in Poland in 1826 and he was raised in a Jewish family before being proselytized by members of the society. In turn, he was persuaded to continue with the work of the society at centres in Europe, the Levant and Africa.

6

By Christmas 1862, the Frankel family and Margaret had settled into their new home in Paris. One wonders what sort of thoughts ran through Margaret's mind that first Christmas away from home? As soon as she stepped out of the front door, she was in a language wilderness. Her English was improving gradually, especially of late, as she had to speak the language constantly, as there was no-one around who spoke Welsh. And now, she had to cope with yet another language. If Margaret was sent on an errand, she would have to communicate in French as few Parisians spoke English. It's no wonder that Margaret became such a competent linguist. By the end of her life, Margaret would have been immersed in several cultures with varying languages. Her time in Paris stood her in good stead.

But although his family made Paris their home, Elias Frankel was constantly travelling. France was a large country and he was often visiting places such as Nantes, Rouen, Amiens, Boulogne, Calais, Lille, Reims, Châlons,

41

Dijon, Lyons and Orléans in France and Ostend, Bruges, Ghent and Antwerp in Belgium, communities where there were a high proportion of Jewish families. The situation in France differed from Britain as France was mainly a Catholic country. The LJS was a Protestant organisation and, as a result, there was as much antagonism between the Protestants and the Catholics as there was between the Protestants and the Jews. Frankel's first report from Paris comments on the 'Romish superstition'.[16] In his two years in France, Frankel distributed 46 Bibles, 95 Pentateuch, 22 Psalters, 49 New Testaments (of which 38 had been sold) and between 800 and 900 tracts. It seems he was proud of his achievements.[17]

Margaret was well aware of her master's work with the Jews, his successes and disappointments. Only one letter from her time in Paris has survived, and this was included at the beginning of her book *Llythyrau Cymraes o Wlad Canaan* [The Letters of a Welsh Lady from Canaan] (1869). The letter gives us an insight into what was of interest to Margaret during her two years in Paris.

Her faith is very important to her and is a familiar lynchpin amongst all that is so unfamiliar to her. Much as her family and friends would do in Rhos, she speaks of the merit of the preachers at the church where she worshipped, the numbers who attended communion and her hopes for the future of the congregation. She is quite outspoken in condemning young French people about their lack of interest in attending any kind of religious service – they preferred going to the theatre or the public house.

She also complains about young French women who forgo nurturing their babies and 'farm' them out to old women in the countryside. These young women have far more interest in eating out and socialising at the opera, and this leaves Margaret with a poor impression of them. It's obvious that Margaret leaves the house quite frequently;

she describes feasts, such as the Festival of the Butchers or the Festival of the Washerwomen. Margaret takes the experiences of Paris in her stride, her observant eyes and curiosity working overtime. She doesn't seem to be homesick for Wales.

Her letters from Paris were a great comfort to her parents in Rhos. Undoubtedly they expected her to return to Wales at some point. But after two years in Paris, with Margaret beginning to familiarise herself with the language and the 'ungodliness' of the French, Elias Frankel announced that he had been offered a post with the LJS at the mother church in Jerusalem.[18] He was keen to move. It was an opportunity which would be difficult for any Christian to refuse.

7

One wonders what went through Margaret's mind this time when she heard the news about yet another move. Did she have a choice to refuse and return to Wales on this occasion? But surely the opportunity to visit Canaan was too attractive to reject? All the religious places she'd read about in the Bible would now come alive to her. Elias Frankel did not know how long he would spend in Jerusalem. But Margaret had already shown that she was an adventurous spirit, therefore it wasn't a difficult decision to make.

Margaret's time in Jerusalem would be documented carefully in the correspondence that she sent home to her family in Rhosllannerchrugog. She would write about once a month, with letters taking a month to arrive in Wales. Most of Margaret's letters were written over the course of a few days, whilst some others were a rushed reply, in order to catch the mail ship before it sailed.

Before too long, Owen Jones came to the conclusion that his daughter's letters were interesting enough for a wider audience to enjoy. Even so, it took three years after Margaret had arrived in Jerusalem for the letters to be published in the Congregationalists' weekly newspaper, *Y Tyst Cymreig* [The Welsh Witness]. Margaret would give her impressions of what it was like to live in a city which was the main religious centre for two-thirds of humanity. Jerusalem was the heart of the monotheist religions, Christianity, Islam and Judaism, and it is very apparent from Margaret's letters that she was not sheltered from the traditions of any faiths in this small city. She would write as leisurely and as comfortably about the rituals of Jews and Muslims in Jerusalem as she would about the Christians. She had quite an extraordinary time in the city.

8

The history of Jerusalem dates back some 3,000 years. The area which we now know of as the 'Old City', and which is less than a square mile, has been destroyed and rebuilt countless times. It has often been said that more suffering and tyranny has occurred over this square mile than any other in the rest of the world. And in history, the following have all fought over Jerusalem: Arabs, Assyrians, Babylonians, Britons, Canaanites, Crusaders, Egyptians, Israelis, Jews, Jordanians, Khwarezmians, Kurds, Macedonians, Mamluks, Ottomans, Palestinians, Persians and Romans. The city has been attacked by the likes of Alexander the Great, Caliph Omar, Herod the Great, Ibrahim Pasha and Nebuchadnezzar.[19]

A small Jebusite (pre-Israelite) tribe was the first to settle there, not far from the present site of the Jewish quarter, around twenty centuries before the birth of Christ. Ten centuries later, the settlement was conquered by the Israelites, under the leadership of King David, who brought the Ark of Covenant to Jerusalem and made it his capital. His son, Solomon, built the First Temple (on the site of the present Temple Mount) around 950 BC. On his death, Jerusalem became the capital of Judea and the twelve tribes of Israel were scattered. The city was conquered by the king of Babylon, Nebuchadnezzar, in 586 BC and the First Temple and the rest of the city were destroyed. The people of Jerusalem were exiled to Babylon for fifty years until the king of Persia, Cyrus, allowed them to return to their homes in Jerusalem.

The Second Temple period in Jerusalem's history commences when the temple was built in around 520 BC. But this rebuilt Jerusalem was short-lived because Alexander the Great conquered the city in 331 BC. Then the Seleucids, Maccabeans and the Hasmonean dynasty took control of Jerusalem until the Romans arrived in around 63 BC.

Herod the Great was installed as ruler of the kingdom of Judea in around 38 BC. On his death, procurators administered the city, with the fifth procurator, Pontius Pilot, ordering the crucifixion of Jesus Christ in around AD 30. Some 36 years later, the Jews revolted against the Romans for the first time, and this led to the destruction of the Second Temple and the torching of Jerusalem. As Jews fled the city, it marked the beginning of the Diaspora of the Jews which lasted for nearly twenty centuries. Jerusalem was destroyed completely by Emperor Hadrian in AD 132, as he feared that the Jews would renew their nationalistic aspirations and would want to return home.

In the year AD 331, Christianity was legalised by the Roman Emperor Constantine. And when Constantine's mother, Helena, visited the Holy Land searching for Christian holy places, it sparked a flurry of church and basilica building. At the beginning of the seventh century, Jerusalem was ruled by the Byzantine Empire, but by the middle of that century a change came about which would last for many centuries to come. Caliph Omar and an Arab army swept into the city under the banner of Islam. This heralded the start of 1,300 years of mainly Muslim rule in a city which had first been Jewish, then a Christian city, but was now an Islamic city. In 688, the Dome of the Rock was constructed on the site of the destroyed temple. The early Islamic leaders granted pilgrimage visits to Jews and Christians until the tenth century. But then, under Caliph Hakim, non-Muslims were cruelly persecuted and churches and synagogues destroyed. These atrocities provoked many in Western Europe to take action and so the Crusade campaigns were launched in the eleventh century.

The Crusaders ruled Jerusalem from 1099 to 1187, when a more moderate administration came to power which allowed Muslims and Jews to settle in the city. The Mamaluks ruled from the 13th to the 16th centuries, but they were defeated by the Ottoman Turks in 1517. The Turks ruled Jerusalem for nearly four centuries and they built the impressive Old City walls. But, in later years, much of the city's infrastructure declined, as buildings and streets were not maintained. An important landmark in Ottoman rule came in 1856. As a result of the Sultan's 'Edict of Toleration', Jews and Christians were allowed to settle in the city once more. Jerusalem came alive. But peace for its 14,000 citizens was far more difficult to achieve.

The British government had always kept a close watch on proceedings in Palestine and on any discussions regarding the future of Jerusalem. Napoléon Bonaparte had already invaded parts of the Middle East in 1798–9, and this had raised shackles in London. The British knew that they would have to get embroiled in the Middle East in order to keep both France and the Russians at arm's length and secure the trade route to India. In 1838 Britain opened a consulate on land adjacent to where Christ Church would later be built by the LJS. Other major European powers followed Britain's example, establishing consulates of their own in the city. By 1840, with the help of the Prussians,

Britain overthrew an Egyptian regime (which earlier had usurped the Ottoman Turkish rule) in Palestine. Members of the LJS now sensed an opportunity to help restore the Jewish people to their homeland. The process was started when an evangelical Protestant Bishopric was established in Jerusalem; the Roman Catholic and the Greek Orthodox churches enhanced their status in Jerusalem also. The first bishop was a former rabbi called Michael Solomon Alexander, and he was the first man of Jewish birth to serve as a bishop in Jerusalem since the city was razed by the Romans in 135. The seat of the new Bishopric would be Christ Church, Jerusalem.

9

The LJS started showing interest in sending missionaries to Jerusalem in 1822. Joseph Wolff, the son of a Bavarian rabbi, was the first of them. At the time, there were 700 Jewish families and five synagogues in the city. He received an encouraging reception whilst circulating copies of the Hebrew New Testament. When asked by a rabbi one time whether good Jews or good Christians were best, his succinct reply was that it was impossible to be a good Jew without believing in Christ. Wolff laid down the groundwork in Jerusalem, and others would follow in his footsteps.[20]

The next step for the LJS was establishing a mission in the city, but there was fierce opposition from the Turks and Roman Catholics. Despite this, a mission was established in 1833. The society anticipated that thousands of Jews would return to their homeland as the political situation changed. However, 1834 was a bad year in Jerusalem as the city had to cope with an earthquake, war, pestilence and famine. These events, however, did not deter the LJS's missionaries from thinking about the location of an English place of worship for the Jews. An appeal was made to raise funds for a Hebrew Christian church and by the end of 1835, £540 had been collected. The proposed plans for the church were in place by January 1837, and an application was made to the Pasha of Egypt, in the name of the British government, for permission to erect a church and mission premises in Jerusalem on a piece of ground on Mount Zion.

After some argument, work commenced in 1841. But there were difficulties ahead, including laying foundation stones in the rocky ground.[21] The first foundation stone was laid by Bishop Alexander in 1842, after digging 35 feet below the level of the ground. But it took another five years to complete the work. Christ Church, Jerusalem was consecrated on 21 January 1849 – exactly seven years after Bishop Alexander commenced his work in Jerusalem but, unfortunately, he had died in 1845. The second Anglican Bishop of Jerusalem was Samuel Gobat. Margaret Jones would mention Bishop Gobat frequently in her correspondence to the family in Rhosllannerchrugog.

Christ Church was situated near one of the main entrances into Jerusalem; Jaffa Gate was not far from the four quarters of the city: Armenian, Christian, Jewish and Muslim. This church was the first modern, international building in Jerusalem. It was built by stonemasons from Malta.[22] At the time, the interior of the church was quite plain. The roof, communion rails, pews and pulpit were imported from Britain. On the eastern side of the church was a stained glass window decorated with the Hebrew words for God, Immanuel, the Spirit of God and an image of a Star of David above a scene of Jerusalem. There were pictures of wheat and vines also. Later, an ornate olive-wood communion table made by the Hebrew Christians in the House of Industry attached to the church was added. And although there were several Greek inscriptions in the church, there were many Hebrew inscriptions also, and a Star and Crown of David in prominent positions. With so much Hebrew to be seen, unsuspecting visitors may have surmised that they'd walked into a synagogue.[23]

However, the Jaffa Gate complex was more than just a church. The society opened other institutions which would help the Jews to 'return'. As mentioned earlier, at the House of Industry Jewish men could learn a trade as well as receive religious instruction. The renowned olive-wood industry, which is now so famous in Jerusalem, began at the House of Industry. In May 1843, the Hebrew College for training Hebrew Christian missionaries was opened. The timetable offered classes in divinity, English, German, Hebrew, arithmetic and music. A book shop and Bible depository was opened in 1844 and also the first modern hospital in Jerusalem in December 1844. Schools for Jewish children were opened too, resulting in a great deal of activity around the complex.

But there was a growing uneasiness from some quarters about the work of the society. Many Jews started to build their own institutions, both medical and educational. Sir Moses Montefiore (a prominent British Jew and the first Jew to receive a knighthood) sent the first Jewish doctor to Jerusalem, with the first Jewish hospital being built in 1854. The LJS had shown the way, and there were plenty of people willing to follow in their footsteps.

10

The work of the society was flourishing when Elias Frankel, his family and Margaret arrived in Jerusalem in January 1865. Elias was employed as a missionary in Jerusalem, but his work meant that he would travel widely across Canaan, as the society had branches in several towns by then.

We get a vivid portrayal of Margaret's character through the letters she sent home to Rhos from the Middle East. The second letter in her book *Llythyrau Cymraes o Wlad Canaan* describes the sea journey from Marseilles to Joppa. It's obvious from the letter that the events she experiences during those weeks travelling between France and Canaan are an absolute eye-opener for her. This was probably the first time that she'd seen Arabs; she describes their dress and mannerisms very carefully. She gets the fright of her life aboard ship in Alexandria in Egypt when she sees a boy, 'an Egyptian (blacker than his brothers)' staring and smiling at her through the porthole, whilst she relaxes alone in her private cabin. She feels very uncomfortable being jostled as she disembarks from the ship in Joppa: 'some of them tried to drag and manhandle us into their boat'. And the journey of some thirty miles, across the mountains from Joppa to Jerusalem is very dangerous. 'The mountains were craggy and steep, with some of the paths as narrow as six or seven inches wide and alongside deep canyons. If our animals had lost their footing, it would have been the end of us, and this made the whole experience terrifying.' So many exciting experiences and Margaret hadn't yet reached Jerusalem.

She describes her home situation in Jerusalem in great detail to her parents back home. She mentions her bedroom and animals such as lizards, and birds such as pigeons which share the room with her. Margaret is a very proud person and she is especially delighted with her room. Despite the uncomfortable description of it, she reassures her family by saying that many people have called it the 'prettiest little room in Jerusalem'. Her daily occupation is to look after the three daughters of the household. She often finds it difficult to allocate time to write letters home, as the girls demand that she reads to them each night. Margaret is also the family maid, and it appears that preparing all the family meals seems to fall on her shoulders too. And although she enjoys the Christmas holidays of 1865, she complains that she has had to prepare the Christmas dinner for a large party because her mistress has 'given up all her daily chores, other than dressing the children'. Food provisions in Canaan excite comment too; she complains about the lack of butter, that the cheese is too salty, that there is no pork and that she can only tolerate jam on her bread. Her beady eyes take especial note of the dress of locals in Jerusalem too. She tells a delightful story about one of the houseboys wearing the clean shirt given to him by his mistress, on top of his dirty clothes.

Margaret is a very popular lady, proof of this being the number of visitors she receives when laid up for several months in a Jerusalem hospital in 1868. Her best friend is a Scottish matron who works at the English Hospital in Jerusalem. Another friend is the mistress of the girls' school in the city. And a rather unexpected friend is a fourteen-year-old boy; he often accompanies her when she visits religious sites, such as the Church of the Nativity in Bethlehem. Margaret would extend a generous welcome to any Welsh visitor who came to the city. She greeted Welsh pilgrims in 1867 and the following year.

When she is not working as a maid or supervising the girls, Margaret is a curious visitor and, unlike today, she gets the opportunity to visit the religious sites of every faith in Jerusalem and the surrounding area. She visits important churches and basilicas, the largest synagogue in Jerusalem and, interestingly, she gets permission to visit the Mosque of Omar (Al-aqsa Mosque today) describing it as 'the prettiest... in Jerusalem'. She describes these holy places very carefully for a readership at home who wouldn't get the pleasure of visiting for themselves.

It is surprising how often Margaret finds herself in the middle of disturbing events during the four years she spends in the Middle East. Less than a year after her arrival in Jerusalem, an outbreak of cholera grips the city. The cholera kills large numbers in the months of November and December 1865, but, as she reassures her parents, the cholera has not killed many Christians. Six months later, a plague of locusts descends on the city, eating everything in sight. The first of May 1866 is a day that Margaret does not forget in a hurry and she makes sure of this by sending a few dead locusts to her parents in her next letter. She shares all this

51

dreadful news with her parents back in Rhosllannerchrugog, without worrying, it appears, about how much her family, thousands of miles away, are worried about her situation. She gives them even more cause for concern when she informs them in February 1867 that the Sultan has ordered the Turks to kill all Christians in Jerusalem. This wasn't an empty threat either: five thousand Christians were slaughtered by the Turks in Damascus in 1861. Margaret's parents probably thought that they would never see their daughter again.

Often, it was not only external disasters such as cholera, locusts and death threats which made Margaret's time in Jerusalem 'interesting'. Margaret, it seems, had the habit of walking into trouble, and shares the whole experience with her parents. Astride an ass or a horse and on her way to a religious site of note, she comes across a few dubious characters. Thankfully, she is always accompanied, but these instances don't seem to bother her at all when 'surrounded by black people of both sexes, [they] started to search my clothing to see how the garments had been made. They didn't wish me any harm, they said, especially if I gave them some *backshish*' (money). Her servant whips her horse and they gallop away from the curious group. Similarly, on a visit to Artas with a friend, she comes across an ugly man, 'half naked, with the few clothes that he had on him, tattered to pieces. His skin was nearly black due to the sun and he was holding a knife in his hand. My companion was frightened witless, but I thought little of it.' Brave Margaret. She speaks to the man in Arabic and Margaret and her companion are allowed to continue their journey unheeded.

It's not surprising then that Margaret suffered from nightmares. One nightmare is described in detail in a letter to her parents. This letter was not published in the book. In fact the state of Margaret's health was a permanent nightmare, especially towards the end of her time in Jerusalem. The state of her health in her first year in Canaan was a secret between her and her brother, John.

She is unwilling for her parents to be told that she suffers from the *ague* for two or three days every three weeks. She admonishes her brother, 'do not mention the fact that I am frequently unwell to anyone, or they might think I was a sickly moaning person'. Margaret suffers, like most of the citizens of Jerusalem, from this disease from time-to-time, as a result of the climate and dust.

Margaret's main health issue is her knee. After several years of trying to negotiate walking along the poor, uneven, rocky city footpaths, Margaret's knee has had enough. She writes in several letters home that she has been nowhere since writing the last letter. By June 1868 the pain in her knee is so bad that she has to be hospitalised. From there she writes the most heart-wrenching letters. She writes of enduring 'more pain in my body in the last three weeks than in the whole of my life'. The opium which she is given to try to ease her pain so that she can sleep is 'the best treasure in the land'. Her knee shows little sign of improving and the doctors recommend that she be repatriated to Britain to receive treatment. She has to travel to Beirut first, as the medical facilities are better there. Margaret is carried on a bed across thirty miles of mountainous passes to Joppa and placed on a ship bound for Beirut. She spends a few weeks there, pleading with the doctors to cut her leg off and give her a cork one instead. 'I think that it would be far better for me to have my leg cut off, because it is of no use to me as it is. But they won't cut it off because, if they did, it would put my life in danger in this hot country.' Her parents, who receive these distressing letters, long to see their daughter returned home to Britain.

At one time Margaret spoke of spending a decade in Canaan. Due to the condition of her knee, Margaret only spent four years in the country. And, as she arrived in Liverpool in early 1869, her dearest wish was to recover quickly so that she could return to the land of milk and honey once more.

PART III

The Letters of the Welsh Lady from Canaan

(These letters have been translated and extensively edited)

I understand also that she is quite capable of describing and writing about what she has seen – which is quite remarkable considering her educational background. I hope and believe that her adventure in publishing the letters will be of advantage to her in more ways than one.

(Thomas Lewis, Bangor; letter of recommendation in *Llythyrau Cymraes o Wlad Canaan*)

Letter I
Written in Paris in 1864
Published 5 June 1868 in Y Tyst Cymreig

Dear Parents

I was surprised that your letter arrived so soon. I was glad to hear that you are all well and I am getting better now too. I have been to chapel each Sabbath since I wrote to you last, back in January. We do not have a regular minister, but we hope to get one soon. The preacher that we have had here for the last three Sabbaths has been the best since I left Wales.

After the sermon we have a prayer meeting, which is a new thing here, and it does show that God is amongst us and giving us his blessings. We are expecting a Jew here next Sunday.

I am beginning to get used to these French people by now, and I do not find anything strange about them anymore. But I do hope that I do not get used to their ungodly ways. They think it foolishness on my part to speak so much about the Bible, religion and the other world, instead of enjoying fatuous pleasures. I do not think much of their empty pleasures and would much rather try to persuade them to experience true faith. Some even ask whether or not there is a heaven.

When we leave chapel on a Sunday, we have to battle to get through the throng of people waiting to enter the entertainment houses. Paris is truly devoted to its foolish pleasures and the young ladies, especially so. After their marriages they rent a small room. This is how they spend their day: they will often buy a penny cake on their way to work and will eat again about eleven, and about six in the evening in large restaurants, spending at least seven and a half pence on the most inexpensive meal. Then they make their way to the opera. If they are mothers, these women will send their baby away to be suckled by an old woman in the countryside, who will be paid about ten pence a year for her trouble. But if they have more than one child, and not enough money, these women tend to stay at home to look after them and go out when they can.

Since your last letter arrived we have had the Feast of the Butchers. Around a hundred men dressed up in the skins of lions and bears, and they wandered around Paris for three days dressed in this fashion. In the middle of the procession was a carriage pulled by six horses. A bullock, completely covered in flowers, rode in the carriage. I have also seen the procession of the Feast of the Washerwomen, which was something very similar, but there is a lady queen instead of a bullock.

I am afraid that I have offended by giving far too much space to the French in this letter – do forgive me this one time. Pity them with all their pleasures.

With my very dearest wishes,
Margaret

Letter II

Written in January 1865
Published 5 June 1868 in Y Tyst Cymreig

Dear Parents

I have written a diary about all the events that happened each day on our journey to Jerusalem. I have written it all as briefly as I can, but do await a better letter next time, because at the moment my time is limited.

Wednesday, 4 January 1865: We have arrived in Dijon, having been on the train for eleven hours and travelled about three hundred miles from Paris. There is much difference in the weather in Dijon. Paris had deep snow, but there is none here, and it is warm. I saw vines planted alongside the railway track.

Thursday, 5 January: We have arrived in Lyon. This town is six hundred miles from Paris and is large and beautiful. We are staying in a spacious hotel, and I have just risen from a most excellent dinner. There were eighteen of us around the table and this was my first proper French dinner. We are to stay here until tomorrow night, when the train leaves Lyon for Marseilles.

Saturday, 7 January: I feel rather lethargic today. We arrived in Marseilles at 7.30 this morning and we have now travelled nearly a thousand miles across France, and have said farewell to the train for a few years perhaps, if not forever, only the Lord knows. We are in a hotel again until Monday, when we leave by ship. This place has one English place of worship, and that belongs to the Church of England. It is not much of a place – around fifty worshippers attend the church, and then it is only half full for a service. The inhabitants of Marseilles are religious in their own way, and follow the Catholic faith.

Monday, 9 January: I have now started a new life living aboard a ship. We departed at three o'clock this afternoon. The ship is quite large and very beautiful. The main room is twenty yards long by ten yards wide and is beautifully decorated. We eat at six o'clock in the evening, but tonight not one of the ladies was able to attend dinner apart from myself. They were all in their beds with seasickness. My mistress was unable to raise her head from the pillow, wishing that she was not suffering, like me. But thanks to good health, I am enjoying this voyage a great deal.

Tuesday, 10 January: We are in Italy and passing the island where Napoléon Bonaparte was born.[1] We then passed the house of Garibaldi too, which, looking through the field-glasses seems to be on an island in the middle of the sea.[2] The sea is quiet at the moment.

Wednesday, 11 January: The ship has docked on the Italian mainland at the town of Uissiaci, but with only a two-hour stop at the port, no one other than the master has gone on to dry land. When he returns, he tells me that the first person he saw was a Welshman from south Wales. Can you imagine how startled I was to hear this fact! We were also told that Garibaldi's picture was to be seen everywhere – on bottles and even on crockery, and all that people speak of is Garibaldi, with people shouting on the streets, 'Long live Garibaldi'. There seems to be little mention of the king.[3]

Thursday, 12 January: We left Italy at eleven o'clock last night, and there is nothing to be seen today but sea and sky. The weather is very pleasant. There are people here from every single tribe, nation and religion and some of them are the strangest people that I have ever seen, not only because of their dress, but also because of how they conduct their daily lives. There are Arabs here who seem to live on the deck – they eat, sleep and do everything there. I was surprised at the fact that they could not pay for somewhere to sleep, and then I saw one of them show another from their party a purse full of gold! They do not eat much, other than some bread drenched in oil and some fruit. One of the Arabs must be very rich, because he brought two servants with him. The rich Arab even had shoes and socks on his feet, and his body was covered in a white silk robe, with a slit up both sides, and a black cloak on his back and something very similar on his head. I would have thought that someone like this would be going first class, but no, he followed the other poorer-looking Arabs onto the deck, much like a sow being attracted to the dung heap.[4]

Friday, 13 January: We are now in view of Mount Etna. Lava runs down all sides of the mountain. It is totally white, but fire and smoke can be seen coming out of the summit.

Saturday, 14 January: The wind is howling today, the waves are rolling, and everybody, including me, has kept to their beds. We saw no land today.

Sunday, 15 January: We have arrived in Alexandria, Egypt and we intend to stay here until Wednesday.

Monday, 16 January: We have changed ships and this one is called the *Godavery*.[5] We go ashore during the day, but return to the ship at night to eat and sleep. But, oh, what an uncivilised place this is! These Egyptians who surround us shout at the top of their voices all day. They are busy unloading our ship, pushing barrels and lifting sacks of nuts, and they sing whilst they do this. But they can only sing five notes, one low and four high ones. And when they sing, they do not all start together in unison, but they join in at random, and they do this *noise* all day.

I was sitting on a chair in my cabin this morning, when suddenly a black cloud darkened my room. When I looked up, I saw an Egyptian (blacker than his brothers) staring at me through the porthole. He was smiling leisurely, but when he saw the terrified look on my face, he slid down his rope a little quicker than he climbed up it, to join his fellow workers in the boat below. They had not been so amused in days. The ship is moored in front of the palace where the governor keeps all his wives. Apparently, he has as many wives as Solomon did. Any man seen going anywhere near the gate to the palace will be put under sentence of death.

Wednesday, 18 January: Here we are, as the Israelites of old, having started our journey from Egypt to Canaan. However we are in far more comfortable circumstances than they, and do not have a hard-hearted Pharaoh chasing us. We have the merciful God to protect us, and one greater than Moses to speak for us. We have not seen the sight of land today and the sea is quiet. We are as comfortable as we ever could be.

Thursday, 19 January: We have arrived in Joppa[6] and have said farewell to the sea for quite some time. A few days ago I found the Egyptians quite uncivil in Alexandria, and the inhabitants of Joppa are just as bad. When our ship moored, we were met by two dozen small boats. Their owners, seeing our large family group, thought us a good catch to get some easy *backshish* (money). They shouted and fought amongst themselves to get their particular boat closest to our ship. As we disembarked, some of them tried to drag and manhandle us by our legs and arms into their boat. When we were finally allowed to choose one of the boats to get us ashore, the unsuccessful boatmen started to swear and curse us, threatening to sink the boat in which we were all sitting if we did not cross over to their boats. Somehow, we all did get to shore safely. We then had to watch the boatmen carry our boxes, and they continued to fight over those as well. It all looked like a never-ending war.

We were eventually met by a friend of my master's, and we went to his house to recover for a few hours. The house was

59

surrounded by orange groves, full of ripe fruits and it was a delightful scene. The sun was quite hot, the weather dry, the ground rock-hard, which was good for the hooves of our horses and donkeys. Joppa itself has buildings which date from the time of Jonah.[7] But it is a very chaotic town today. The roads are very narrow and stony, and it is impossible for any carriage to travel along them. We happened to arrive at the house of my master's friend on washing day. In the backyard there were three women doing the washing. Their heads were lapped in a sheet, with only their eyes, noses and mouths in view. They sat there in the dirt, in the midst of all the wet, and used a wooden platter to wash the clothes, not a bowl. Their small children played around them, wearing only some scraps of clothing about their bodies. As I was staring at this scene, a man came into the yard with a straw mat, placed it on the ground, took off his cloak and put that on the mat with other items of headwear. He then stood on all of this, raised both his hands and face skyward for about three minutes, then bowed onto his knees, with his face towards the ground, to worship his prophet.

We left Joppa at about four o'clock in the afternoon, and then arrived at Ramle,[8] which was a place once known as Arimathea, the old home of Joseph, the kind gentleman who buried our Lord in his own new grave.[9] By this time it was eight o'clock at night and, as you can imagine, having ridden for hours, we were glad to get to the monastery which would be our lodging house for the night. But when we arrived everything was locked up, with the monks having gone to bed. We had great trouble rousing one of them, but we did eventually and had a reasonable supper there.

Friday, 20 January: We have arrived in Jerusalem at last. We were so tired, having been riding from seven o'clock in the morning until six o'clock in the evening, enduring the heat of the day. The first two hours of the morning were not too bad. But the heat became more and more intense as we crossed into the mountains, which were difficult for the animals to pass through. The mountains were craggy and steep, with some of the paths only six or seven inches wide and alongside deep canyons. If our animals had lost their footing, it would have been the end of us, and this made the whole experience quite terrifying. The screams of the young children as we travelled along these narrow paths attracted the attention of some Arabs who lived in holes in the mountains (holes similar to those which sheep use as a refuge in the mountains of Wales). Near-naked Arab women came to the entrances of the holes to see what was going on. They had their babes in arms, and they all looked as uncivilised as each other.

One of the missionaries from Jerusalem came out to meet us with lunch and, at about one o'clock, we dismounted our animals and sat in the shade of an olive tree. Oh how wonderful it was to taste a little water after such an experience. And if only we had been able to see somewhere in which Christ had trodden, it would have been even better. I have to say that it is far more pleasing to read of the adventures of others who visit these parts, than to do it yourself. But I think all the pain will make it worthwhile in the end.

An hour after leaving the olive tree, we came across Ciriath-jearim, where God's ark rested for three months.[10] More Christians from Jerusalem came to meet us, some on donkeys, others on horses and some on foot. We had recognised them from a distance as they all wore black garments. As we approached Jerusalem, I did see some two or three dozen examples of those underground potato stores that we have in our gardens in Wales. But instead of storing potatoes, it seems that people live in these, and many of these together are thought of as being villages.

Margaret

Letter III
Written Spring 1865
Published 31 July 1868 in Y Tyst Cymreig

Dear Parents

You mentioned in your last letter that my letters were taking a long time to arrive, but I did send you one by return when yours arrived. I do know that John's last letter took a month to arrive. I am glad to hear that my letters are so interesting to you, but I do not think that they are good enough to be published as a book. But if you really do think that they are worthy of publication, I hope, dear parents, that the readers will forgive all the mistakes and weaknesses in them. Please do not think of publishing anything which will not be of a little benefit to someone.

Now for some news. The roads of Jerusalem are now empty, as the crowds of pilgrims have left the city, now that Easter has passed. Pilgrims have been arriving in Jerusalem since the week before Christmas, with hundreds here in the fortnight before Good Friday to visit the Church of the Holy Sepulchre. It has been quite impossible to travel through all the crowds. Many pilgrims try to be in the city on Good Friday in particular, because they think that a 'fire' will come down from heaven.

At daybreak, the elderly and infirm will gather at the safest and most convenient places in the Church of the Holy Sepulchre, before the crowds start arriving at ten o'clock. But there will still be another four hours before the ceremony starts. At two o'clock in the afternoon, the church will fall silent (other than for the occasional heavy sigh from someone knocking someone else accidentally in the back, or an elbow jostling someone, or from being unable to move at all: the place will be that full). Then, the high-priest will appear and stand in the doorway of the room in which it is thought that Jesus Christ died. He will then take all but one of his garments off (for modesty's sake), to show that there is nothing deceitful about him. He will then enter the room to pray for the 'fire' to come down from heaven and appear to the congregation. They will be highly excited and expectant by now. When the 'fire' finally appears from under the marble coffer, the crowd will surge to get to the appointed place as though their lives depend on it, and if someone dares shout out 'Take care', the riposte will be that no-one was ever burnt by this fire before. The pilgrims will have brought a short piece of rope with them, and they will rush towards the fire and ignite the rope. Then they will place a night cap over the burnt end of the rope, which in turn blackens the cap. These caps will later be packed away in their cases, ready to be taken back home to their country of origin. When the pilgrim dies, friends will be told that the pilgrim will want to have the cap on his head in his coffin, so that when the day of resurrection comes, those who own the blackened caps will be recognised as those who were meant to be saved.

The poor things, I say, to be deceived by the priest in such a way. How can they practice such a fraud, filling the hearts and minds of men with such untruths? But God is the greatest Judge; He is capable of reprisal.

You may like to know under what circumstances these people commence their pilgrimages. Those members of the Greek Orthodox Church who decide to go on a pilgrimage must make the fact known to their priest and the congregation of their church. Then, the priest collects money from the congregation to contribute towards the expense of the pilgrimage. Those who contribute the most feel themselves to be as important as the person going on the pilgrimage, as they have done a good deed. The most generous contributors have the right to demand a blackened cap from the pilgrim on his return.

Just prior to the pilgrim leaving for Jerusalem, he is led to the church where the priest prays that all the saints will look after him on his journey. Some of the money offered is for journey costs, and the rest is for the church and the covenants.

When he arrives in Joppa, he will go to the Greek convent where he will pay 26 piastres (which are five shillings) for lodgings, and the same again will happen at Ramle. He will have a letter of recommendation for all the churches. The following day, the pilgrim will reach Jerusalem and will, with tears running down his face, make his way immediately to the Church of the Holy Sepulchre and kiss every inch of the grave of Jesus. If only the poor pilgrims knew better of these fearsome superstitions.

Other pilgrims' first impressions of Jerusalem are to stand and stare at one of the gates for quite some time before entering. And then they feel the need to touch every notable stone until they reach the convent. After taking refreshments, they will be led to the convent's church, where the priest will pray for the pilgrim. The pilgrim's feet will then be washed and all pilgrims will assemble in a large room, where the high-priest records in a book their names and the names of those who offered money to finance the pilgrimage. The high-priest will then ask each pilgrim how many family members are alive and how many are dead. The pilgrim has to pay twenty shillings for all members of the family who are alive and ten shillings for all members who are dead. (Those who are rich have to pay more.) The pilgrim later receives a token for each member of the family.

The pilgrim leaves the convent the following day and is met by a man who collects the tokens and another three shillings and sixpence. This pays for a later visit to the river Jordan. But before that, there is much to see, such as the Church of the Holy Sepulchre, where the pilgrim will write his name in the book (for the payment of another five shillings). He will then sleep that night at the church, and this will be regarded by his fellow countrymen as being particularly virtuous. On the fifth day of his visit to Jerusalem, he will be escorted to the Garden of Gethsemane and then to the church where it is thought that Mary was buried (and all for just another five shillings). He will next make the journey to Bethlehem and visit all the churches and convents in the place, paying five shillings for the privilege at each one.

There are other sorts of *pilgrims* who come to Canaan and it would be an absolute blessing if they stayed at home. Their only objective in coming to Jerusalem is so that everybody knows that they have been here. The only place of interest to them is the tavern, and I am afraid to say that these places are full to the brim from February until May. It would be wonderful if Jerusalem were free of this malediction and did not have a single ale house.

I did not want to tire you with a lengthy letter, so do forgive me. I promised you the story of my visit to the river Cedron and I shall do that very briefly. We travelled through the valley of Ben-hinnom, where Manasseh drove his sons through the fire (2 Chronicles 33). Nearby is the field which was bought for the thirty pieces of silver. It does not look anything like a field today, but more like a high crag, two hundred feet higher than the footpath. The crag is full of caves, within which are the graves of unknown men killed in a war a few years after Christ rose to heaven. About half a mile further on is Enrogel (2 Samuel 17) which is near the river Cedron. This has a deep well.

We came to the river Cedron, but I was very disappointed as I had hoped to see the river overflowing as I had heard so much about it. But, if you took two gallons of water and poured it into the river bed – well, that is the amount of water we saw in the Cedron that day. Hundreds of people from Jerusalem had come to see it and were also disappointed. Seeing plenty of water in the river Cedron is very important to the local inhabitants, as it is a sign that there will be enough water in the summer. The water that we did see was not that clear, but it was good to drink. We also saw three or four Jews there, praying in memory of King David.

I must end now. This from your dearest daughter, who is healthy and comfortable,

Margaret

Letter IV
Written 16 May 1865
Published 19 June 1868 in Y Tyst Cymreig

Dear Parents

I took an outing one afternoon to the Mount of Olives, and my main reason for going was to see the Garden of Gethsemane. I can see the Mount of Olives from the rooftop of our house. We left Jerusalem through Joppa Gate and came across many lepers begging for money in a most distressing way. They wished us every blessing if we would give them some money. The only clothes they wore were ripped cloaks and red caps on their heads, with calico or cotton rolled around it.

When we reached the foot of the Mount of Olives, where the Garden of Gethsemane is located, I felt too tired to walk any further. So I sat on a large stone at the side of the garden until the family returned from the mountain. But oh, my dear parents, I could not but shed a few tears there, whilst thinking about my Saviour and all his suffering.

The section of the garden where it is thought that Jesus suffered the most is decorated with trees and very beautiful flowers. You have to pay the man who looks after the garden to enter this part. The weather was hot on the day that we went to Gethsemane, without a cloud in the sky, apart from one cloud, which hovered right above the garden. That cloud was as black as could be and, as I looked at it, I thought of the cloud of indignation of the just Lord, when it rained on his dear and only-begotten Son, so that the way could be opened to guilty sinners.

When the family rejoined me in the Garden of Gethsemane we walked along the path it is thought that Jesus was led by to the court of the high-priest. There is now a hospital there and this has been built on the ruins of the old debating house. A nearby bridge is thought to be one that Jesus went under on his way to being crucified.

On our journey home we passed Bethesda lake, which is now enclosed in a garden belonging to a family of Muslims. A wall surrounded the garden, with doors here and there, through which we could see the lake. The lake was completely dry at the time, and is so for three-quarters of the year, apparently.

Religion is the main topic of conversation for the residents of Jerusalem these days. The Protestants have a prayer meeting each morning at six o'clock and at half-past four on Tuesday and Friday afternoons, another every Saturday night, and a meeting at four o'clock on a Sunday afternoon. Only two of these meetings are in English.

A man here called Mr Saphira[11] preaches the gospel as boldly as Paul ever did, in my opinion. He is not a missionary by vocation, but carries out the work of a missionary to all intents and purposes. He also sells books for the society in London, and when he gets the time, he looks for verses in the Bible to show the Jews that Jesus is the Messiah.

The Muslims kneel at four o'clock each morning shouting 'God is great'. They are called to prayer three times a day and, at the hour of prayer, it is prohibited for the Turks to do anything. As soon as the call to prayer comes, hundreds of them are seen on the roof tops of houses praying. The Armenians are also very zealous in their own ways. At sunset, you will see many of the older Armenians taking bundles in their arms to sleep at the burial site of our Lord, because they think that the grave belongs to them.

We have had very little rain in Jerusalem so far this year, and there may be a shortage of water. The locusts have also ruined all the crops that were sown. They descend in great clouds for two to three hours each day, appearing like a snowstorm, darkening the sky and hurting our eyes.

There have been many visitors from several different parts of the world in Jerusalem this year. Some come into the city with a crown of thorns on their heads, in remembrance of our Lord. I assume that you have read in the newspapers that Prince Arthur has been a visitor.[12] We had the pleasure of seeing him every day when he was in Jerusalem. He came to our church here on the Sabbath. He looks quite young and seems an affable young man; he smiled cheerfully at everybody.

I must end now, hoping that you are all well,
Margaret

Letter V

Written 15 July 1865
Published 26 June 1868 in Y Tyst Cymreig

Dear Parents

I received your letter on the 20th of last month and I was delighted to hear that I had a new brother. My master's daughters have requested to see a photograph of him as soon as possible. I am glad to hear that my mother is now recovering after the birth.

But I was so saddened to hear of the deaths of several young people, one of them being my close friend, Joseph Jones. I hope that his death will mean that his friends find God. And I was surprised to hear that Mrs Williams has had twins. I hope that they will be of great comfort to her.

I have not been anywhere since the last time I wrote. Therefore, I am going to give you some news about my home and describe the house that I live in. The only house of comparable size to this one, that I know of, is the house of Mr Owen, Aberderfyn. There is a garden in front of the house, which measures twenty yards by seven yards. Three rooms face the garden and the room in the middle reminds me of the room where the invalid was lowered through the ceiling to be healed by Jesus.[13] This middle room is eight yards by eight with three- to four-foot wide walls surrounding it. There are no stairs inside the building, but there are steps outside which go up onto the roof. The roof is flat and made for walking on.

My own room measures a yard and three-quarter in width and is two and a half yards in length. Two donkeys live in the next room (and they are only separated from me by paper on the upper half of the partition). I am most pleased that these donkeys behave very well at night. On the other side of my room twenty pigeons or doves have their accommodation. A few weeks ago, there were around twenty-five of them, with the twenty-fifth being called the King of the Doves because he was much more beautiful than the others and, as a result, had earned the respect of the rest of the doves. However, a big black dog put paid to the 'King' and four other doves.

On the other side of my room, in some sort of a cellar, with a grate to let a little light and air in, live twenty-one hens and a young cockerel. The young cock makes the most dreadful noise. Perhaps he was taken from the land of his fathers before he was taught to sing!

There is one small glazed window in my room – yet this window is four times the size of windows back home in Wales. The window is situated above my bed. Other lodgers in the room with me are four- to five-inch long lizards. They fall off the trees in their sleep and end up in my room. But I do not want you to think that I live in some sort of sty either. Some of the adults who have seen the inside of my room claim that it is the prettiest small room in Jerusalem.

I seem to have come to the end of my letter without writing down half of what I had intended to say. If you like this homely news, do say, and you can have the other half of the story of the neighbourhood and neighbours in the next letter.

From your dear daughter,

Margaret

Letter VI
Written 3 October 1865
Published 3 July 1868 in Y Tyst Cymreig

Dear Parents

You have no idea how delighted I was to receive your letter. I read it at least half a dozen times on the day of receipt – it renewed my spirit, body and soul, especially when I read of the old chapel and its meetings, of the ministers and everybody in the old country who are so dear to me.

Last Monday, I had the same privilege as Mary Magdalene and Mary, mother of James, when I was asked to visit the place where our Lord lay. I felt so undeserving of experiencing the same privilege as those two devout women. A church was built over the site of the grave a few centuries ago, and I have come to understand recently that four religious sects worship there. The church is divided into four sections and there is a bridge connecting the different parts. The most opulent section of the church belongs to the Russians. It is decorated in the most elaborate way, with a gallery decked in gold gilt, the altar full of the most exquisite gold and silver cups and bowls, and candlelight radiating about the room. A ceremony was taking place during our visit. Young boys carried candles and the high-priest appeared, dressed in a scarlet robe with a crown of gold and silver on his head, and holding dozens of necklaces. With his white hair and beard, the high-priest reminded me of Aaron.[14] Other priests then took part in the ceremony, carrying what I thought looked like a sugar basin made of gold; others carried intricately decorated small chests. They all walked up and down the length of the church many times.

I wanted to know where the grave of Jesus was, and was told that it was in a small room but three feet away from where I was standing. I watched others taking their shoes off and, as a mark of respect, I did the same so that I could take a closer look at the marble coffer that Jesus lay under. The room was covered in valuable and precious gifts left by earlier pilgrims, and not a single inch of the coffer had escaped from being kissed by pilgrims over the centuries. I was then led a short distance to visit the place where it is thought that Jesus was moved to after he died on the cross. Many lanterns of all colours adorn that site too.

Later we made our way to Calvary, where the crucifixion took place. I felt quite weak and afraid, standing in the very place where our blessed Saviour was led, like a lamb to the slaughter, spat at and subjected to derision.[15] Yet I also felt as though I wanted to stay there forever, so that I could think about Jesus's suffering instead of the empty thoughts that fill my mind on a daily basis. Do pray for me, so that I keep to the thoughts I had at that time.

We then moved on to the place where it is thought that Jesus was flogged and whipped before being crucified. Other than a small image in stone, this place is largely ignored now and has the dust of centuries on it. We then descended the twenty-five steps down to a cellar, where the crucifix is said to be buried. Nearby is a rock with a fissure running through it and, according to the citizens of Jerusalem, this rock was cleaved on the day of our Lord's death.[16] Not everybody believes this, but I will make what I will of it, as you can. I do hope you have not tired of reading about my visits, that is, if you understand what I have said.

Since writing the last time I have been to visit the graves of the kings of Israel. They lie around half a mile outside the gates of Jerusalem. It was quite an ordeal getting to see them, as I had to bend down double to enter into the caves where the graves were located. There were many carvings around the cave, which now look the worse for wear. The bodies of the kings lay under a stone in a small room within the cave. The place was candlelit, as many Jews go there at night to sleep amongst the graves.

I must end now, with warmest wishes to all my friends and relatives, hoping that they are as healthy as I am.

From your daughter,

Margaret

Letter VII

Written 3 October 1865
Published 7 August 1868 in Y Tyst Cymrieg

My Dear Brother

I am quite ashamed that it has taken me so long to write to you. I am sure that you will forgive me and show the love that you have towards your sister.

I have but a very poor excuse, and that is to do with your request for me to find out the distance between Jerusalem and Bethania and tell you in my next letter. I did try to persuade someone to come with me to Bethania, because it is dangerous travelling on your own in this country. I asked the mistress of the city's girls' school three times, but her excuses were: firstly, that she'd promised to go somewhere else; secondly, that the weather was too warm and thirdly, that she did not feel well enough to ride the distance. Therefore, dear brother, I have failed in my attempt to visit Bethania to get an answer for you.

I have little other news, other than to say that I am ill for two or three days every three weeks or so with the *ague*. I'm unsure what the *ague* is translated into Welsh, but my

Welsh dictionary says *cryd y durthion y wrach*.[17] Most of the citizens of Jerusalem suffer from this disease (but please John, do not mention the fact that I am frequently unwell to anyone, or they might think I was a sickly moaning person). However, other than the days on which I am unwell, I am completely healthy and happy and I look better than I have ever done. If only you were to come to Jerusalem to see me one day, you would agree with me also. I wish that you could see me galloping my mistress's mule over the mountains of Judea, with the brim of my hat turned inside out and my hair flowing loose because my hat pin cannot keep it secure. My hair has a habit of dancing on my shoulders in the most felicitous way these days. If only you could be there with me, riding the master's horse, and we could visit so many places together.

I would be very glad indeed to hear that you had embraced the beliefs of Jesus and love Him to such an extent that you would find dear the ground upon which He once walked.

I have been to see Calvary, and the place where Jesus was buried and have also seen the burial site of the kings of Israel. Since you live in Rhos, you need to go and read the letter I sent (at the same time as this one) to my parents, which will tell you all about my visit.

The weather has been very dry. We have had no rain for five months and there is no sign that we are going to get any either. And the butter has gone the same way as the rain. We have seen none of that, let alone tasted any, for the past three months. I cannot eat the cheese at all, as it is too white, too dry and too salty. And as for pork, there is not even a word of getting any and buying beef is also difficult. And so the only spread that I can tolerate on my bread is different varieties of jam.

I must end now, do remember me kindly to all my friends.

From your dear sister,
Margaret

Letter VIII
Written 13 December 1865
Published 10 July 1868 in Y Tyst Cymreig

Dear Parents

Thank you for your letter and other gifts which I received on the third of this month. It was wonderful to see the faces of all my friends in the photographs. Do thank Mr E Lettsome[18] especially for taking them on my behalf. By return, I send him these flowers which are little repayment really for his kind gift. Could he also take a photograph of my uncle and aunt Phillips, Stryd-y-gof? My mistress and the children cannot believe how many friends and relatives I have.

I have not been anywhere recently and it is not because I have been unwell, but because there has been a cholera outbreak in the city. The Jews have fled the city in their hundreds, and many of them died in the mountains from fear and tiredness, as they escaped the ailing city with very little, and left their animals (which could have carried them safely across the mountains) at home. The military have fled the city also, leaving the place in a right old state. They opened the gates of all the prisons before they left, letting bad (and some of the good) prisoners out. No good can come of that, surely.

I have heard of great suffering in the city, especially in the houses of those afflicted by the disease. Crying and screaming, day and night – enough to make me think that the destruction of Jerusalem was about to happen for a second time. Our Turkish neighbours were seen eating their breakfasts in the backyard of their house one morning at 8 o'clock. By 4 o'clock in the afternoon on the same day, the family had not only been killed by cholera, but each family member had been buried as well. But then dear parents, *we* are all alive and well here, and it seems that the Protestants of the city have been saved, as only one Protestant man has died as a result of the outbreak.

I will describe the burial of our nearest neighbour, who died leaving four wives and goodness knows how many children to mourn after him. One morning, before daybreak, when we had become used to hearing the screaming coming from down the road, we heard the screaming coming from a house much closer to ours, and this scared the children and me. We went onto the roof of the house and when the mourning ladies saw us, they came up onto the roof as well, clenching their front teeth with their fingers as though they wanted to pull their teeth out of their jaws. Then, they sat on the floor, took out a handkerchief, lifted it above their heads and started to rip it to shreds.

At the funeral itself, the women screamed for half an hour at a time and later, a woman unknown to the deceased appeared, and she was paid to do all sorts of howling and screaming. Musicians arrived and, in a while, the body came out of the house, not in a coffin, but draped in some sort of sheet. The body was then taken to the mosque, and later it was buried in the man's own back garden in front of a hundred and twenty mourners shouting 'Hurrah' and jumping up and down as the body was lowered into the ground. This part of the ceremony was known as 'The Derby's Dance', apparently.

I wish I were able to give you more interesting stories, but I have been nowhere recently.

This, imperfectly from your daughter,

Margaret

Letter IX

Written 23 January 1866
Published 14 August 1868 in Y Tyst Cymreig

My Dear Brother

I should have replied to you much sooner, but do not believe for one moment that I have not been thinking of you. It is lack of time which has prevented me from writing sooner, as the young girls have persuaded me to read to them each evening, and that has now become a matter of course as soon as the servant clears the table.

Well John, the first [Christmas] holidays in Jerusalem have been very interesting (and something very similar to the workers' events that you describe in your letter). My master and mistress held a tea party to all sixty proselytes on the day following Christmas Day. After the tea, colourful magic lanterns were hung everywhere and the children were very excited. There was music and laughter, with the music played by the church organist. We sang Psalm 111 and the 'Hallelujah Chorus' in Hebrew. I had never heard such a heavenly sound. Later, all the children went into an adjoining room and discovered their gifts by the tree: aprons for the girls and wooden toys for the boys.

On Christmas Day itself, there had been a sermon at the church at ten in the morning and at three in the afternoon. A lunch was laid out afterwards, and many of the master and mistress's friends attended. But, unfortunately, I was the one who had to prepare all the food. I have to say that my mistress has given up all her daily household chores, other than dressing the children in the morning. But I am not complaining, as the past six months have been the happiest of my life so far. I have made a remarkable number of friends and when I go to visit these friends, *I* am waited upon hand and foot, by *their* servants and am rather ashamed to receive such treatment! My very best friend is the matron who works at the English hospital in Jerusalem. She comes from Scotland originally, but she has married a returning Jew – they have three children, the eldest being seven years old.

I have another special young friend too, who is the son of a missionary. He is fourteen years old, and his mother died when he was but five years old. His father is his only living relative. He comes to visit our house as soon as school is finished for the day. I worry that this will not be for much longer, as there is talk of him being sent away to college in the summer. I shall miss him, because he comes with me wherever I go.

The weather has been quite wet for the past six weeks in Jerusalem and when it does rain here, it rains in torrents. There is no such thing as drizzle in Canaan, but deluges of rain, when it eventually comes. One day an Arab girl who sells milk came to the door and I asked her what she wanted. She said, 'Rejoice.' 'Why?' I replied. 'Because the river Cedron has burst its banks.' This is a sure sign to the inhabitants that there will be enough water in Jerusalem throughout the hot summer ahead. Many people go to see the river when it overflows, and we are thinking of going there on the next fine day.

But, to finish the story of the Arab girl. After she had said her news, she still stood on the doorstep laughing. I did not know what she was laughing about. I showed her the door and said to her *masalame*, which means 'go in peace'. But peace or not, the girl would not move an inch, and when I asked her what she wanted, she laughed even more and said *backshish*. So I gave her some pudding in a bowl, which was so hot that she did not know what to do with it. I then gave her a spoon – she was frightened of that, and eventually ended up eating the pudding with her fingers!

All this from your dear sister,
Margaret

Letter X

Written 18 March 1866
Published 21 August 1868 in Y Tyst Cymreig

Dear Parents

I received your letter on 20 February, having long waited for it. I hope you write sooner next time.

You asked me in your last letter how I felt about staying in Jerusalem for another nine years. Well, all I can say is that the last year has been one of the happiest of my life, and were I only to be sure that I would see everyone I knew in Wales at the end of that nine years, then I would have no objections to staying here.

I suspect that you may be waiting for news about Bethlehem in this letter. The first place that we visited on our journey to Bethlehem was a large convent, built a few centuries ago on the site where Elijah was fed by the raven.[19] Nowadays, it accommodates pilgrims and there is an excellent view of both Jerusalem and Bethlehem from there. We did not go inside, as there were large dogs loose about the place, which was enough to deter anyone from entering.

Having ridden for another half an hour, we came to the grave of Rachel.[20] There is a large column on her grave, and there were three or four Arabs praying and kissing her grave. All Arabs regard visiting her grave as an obligation during their lifetime.

We arrived in Bethlehem some twenty minutes later. Neither of us knew where the Church of the Nativity was, so we procured the service of a local boy who, in my opinion, could not have been more than twelve years old. He wore a tatty shirt, which came down to his knees. This boy had been following us for a while and, to be honest, we would have done better not to accept his service as once we got to the church door, we were met by a horde of young boys, and we did not know how to get rid of them. The church doorkeeper would not allow more than three boys to accompany us into the church. So the rest of them went round to the other doors of the church, knocking on them loudly, shouting in Arabic that the young gentleman and his wife (that is, my thirteen-year-old friend and I!) needed assistance in looking at the church. They did not get very far and when we left, the horrid boys who had noticed that it was I who carried a purse in my hand, came up behind my donkey, made the most ridiculous noises, which startled the donkey and me.

Inside the Church of the Nativity, we descended twenty steps into the cellar where the manger lies. It certainly was not the same manger as in Jesus's day, as this one was made of marble. Inside the manger was some sort of cradle which held a wax carving of a little boy dressed in clothing decorated with gold, silver and pearls. These expensive items also hung from the ceiling. Dozens of colourful candles and valuable artefacts have been left by pilgrims over the years. The cradle is only taken out of the manger once a year, at Christmas time. Very many people visit then and it is well-nigh impossible to push through and get a view of the manger, apparently. Many pilgrims think that life comes to this effigy for a short while each Christmas Day, so they visit in order to worship and to kiss the man who carries the cradle. But honestly, just standing on the place where Jesus was born is enough to be shown His true love. We do not really need to worship images. There was a white stone next to the manger and this signified where Mary sat as baby Jesus suckled. It is said that nursing mothers, who do not have enough milk for their own babies will lay both their hands on this white stone, and then it is thought they will have enough milk to feed their babies.

This church is the only beautiful place in Bethlehem. The rest of the town is totally disorganised. The roads are steep, narrow and dirty with many a skeleton of a cat or dog lying on the roads every two to three yards.

On the eastern side of the church lies the ground where

the angel appeared to the shepherds. I do not know why they call them shepherds' fields. They are the strangest looking fields that I have ever seen, and very different to what we have at home in Wales. These fields are just mountainous scrub, with little soil to be seen and no hedges either. Unlike at home, there are no rushes, heathers or bilberries. These fields are very bare and rocky and probably cursed, just like the people.

On our way home we visited Gihon lake where Solomon was anointed king.[21] The lake, which is surrounded by a wall, has only a few inches of water in it, despite it being winter time. Many Turks bury their dead around the lakeshore.

I see there is little space to write anymore. Do send my regards to my friends and family.

From your daughter,

Margaret

Letter XI

Written 13 August 1866
Published 18/25 September 1868 in Y Tyst Cymreig

Dear Parents

Having waited for ten days full of hope for your letter and, as a response, half-written the most pitiful letter that anyone ever wrote, because I genuinely thought that something dreadful had happened, I received your letter on 30 July. I had spilt many a tear by then, and now I have spilt many a tear of joy at getting your letter. It was interesting to read your account of the yearly meeting and the eisteddfod. I only wish we had something similar here in Jerusalem.

Now for a few accounts of how I have spent my time. As you can see, I have sent you some locusts. These devastating creatures have been flying some twenty feet above ground for the best part of the month of April, and the Misses Frankel and I had been out on the mountains looking for locusts to send to you, quite unaware of what was about to happen.

During the 1st of May, an unforgettable day for the people of Assyria, we were woken by the sound of locusts. We really do think that that day was the enactment of the prophecy of Joel.[22] The sound of the locusts lasted from five o'clock in the morning until seven in the evening. The only other noises to be heard were the screams of women. Some women sat on the ground, dressed only in an item of rag clothing, rocking backwards and forwards until they were completely exhausted. They were covered in locusts, and for some relief they would shake the branch of an olive tree – but the locusts seemed to be gummed to the women and the trees. Many women thought their life's work was ruined, and even took to throwing soil over their heads and shouting that the days of famine were here. Even the soldiers refused to play their musical instruments that day. They all walked around in a daze, sure that they were in the presence of God and, as Joel had said in 2:6, were afraid to open their mouths.

The locusts got into the houses and jumped on the table amongst the food. We thought that we would never get rid of them, yet miraculously, by the following morning, as it said in Exodus [10:19], they had virtually disappeared. Read the book of Joel. It is exactly as it happened there.

I went to Bethania a while ago, but I did not get the chance to tell you about it. I had left the city through Joppa Gate, but as I went past Damascus Gate, I was surrounded by black people of both sexes, who started to search my clothing to see how the garments had been made! They did not wish me any harm, they said, especially if I gave them some *backshish*. I was not too sure about this, but thankfully my servant whipped my horse which made it gallop through my tormentors. We were left unhindered then until we reached the bottom of the Mount of Olives, where my friends were waiting for me.

We dismounted our animals and walked up the Mount

of Olives. As we approached the summit, we sat down and looked at the view of Jerusalem. We stood not far from where Jesus had wept for the city and its inhabitants.[23] There is a wonderful view of Jerusalem from here: you can see all the strong fortresses and the mosques where the Turks shout 'It is better to pray than sleep' at four o'clock every morning. (They do this another three times during the day, but replace the word 'sleep' with 'eat'.) But the most beautiful building to be seen from this vantage point is the Mosque of Omar, which is built on the foundations of the temple that Solomon built. It is surrounded by a platform, but you have to pay a pound to enter, unless you have a ticket from the Pasha.

There is a small village at the summit of the Mount of Olives. But nobody seems to have been round to clean it for centuries, and of all the dirty places I have been to, this must be the dirtiest. Those who lived there were just as filthy, if not worse. Some of the men just wallowed in the dust, and others sat like tailors with four to five yards of pipe coming out of their jaws.[24] The women also sat in a row in the dust, and their children played in the dirt. As we approached, the men took their pipes out of their mouths and started staring and laughing at us. We then turned to leave and were rather glad to do so, although the children followed us for quite a while, teasing our mules and horses with pinpricks.

On our descent from the Mount of Olives to Bethania we saw the river Jordan and the Dead Sea. Bethania is in a little valley in the middle of the hills and looks a rather insignificant village, with only thirty to forty houses. Some of these houses are so low in the ground that some visitors end up trampling over them, without realising that people live there. As we entered the village we were met by an old man, who placed his hand on his forehead to indicate respect, then on his heart to indicate love and then on his lips to denote a holy kiss. After giving us some candles, he led us down some steps to a cave, which is known as the tomb of Lazarus.[25] There, you can see a portion of a wall which denotes the place where Lazarus rose from the dead at our Lord's command. I was so glad to see all these places. I must close now.

Your dearest daughter,
Margaret

Letter XII
Written 13 October 1866
Published 2 October 1868 in Y Tyst Cymreig

Dear Parents

I was delighted to receive a letter from you on 30 September, a week earlier than expected. I was so pleased to hear that Mr [Robert] Thomas, Bangor, had won such a prize.[26] Indeed, this is a most remarkable feat, as a chair made out of oak from Twm o'r Nant's house is more extraordinary, perhaps, than water from the river Jordan. I hope he has a long and healthy life to enjoy the chair.

I have not been anywhere recently, so I am going to take the opportunity to give you news from home. I have described the house and garden to you before. The garden gate opens out onto the courtyard of the church, which is called Christ Church on Mount Zion. This is such a dear name, is it not, and a church on Mount Zion is mentioned in Zechariah 8:3. That particular chapter promises much for this city, and we long for the time when everyone will behold His glory.

The courtyard is about sixty feet long and thirty feet wide and is surrounded by a few trees, but there are no graves here as you would see in the graveyards of the Church of England. There is a lodge next to the church also, and that is where a family of proselytes live. At the end of the courtyard is a gateway which leads out to a road, the like of which you would never see in Wales: if you stand in the middle of it, you can place both hands on the walls of the buildings on both sides. The road is very craggy and narrow and you have to be very careful not to fall over and hurt yourself – walking on it could lead to serious harm. This is the state of roads in Jerusalem these days.

When you come to the end of the road, on the left, you will see the Tower of David, which is where the Turkish military are stationed. And not too far away is the market hall which is *not* a beautiful building full of all good things, positioned in the most sensible way. No, Jerusalem does not have such a place. The market's floor is a series of craggy steps and everybody sits on these, whether it is summer or winter. Some of the vendors sell their goods in baskets, but there are others who place their goods for sale on dirty rags. Everything looks old and tatty, so old in fact that I can hardly believe that some of the goods were once new. The women in the market hall wear a narrow short gown with wide sleeves, so that they can carry their goods to market. They also carry a sack, which often holds their baby. And on their heads, they wear a cloth which was once white. The men wear just a shirt, with a large belt about their waist and a red cap. They never seem to wear socks and are forever showing their knees. You cannot imagine the noise that is made in the marketplace, between the donkeys, children, camels (several dozen of them), men shouting and buyers and sellers all falling out with one another. And women's voices cry above everything else. The marketplace in Jerusalem is not the most pleasant place in the world.

I must end now. This, from your dear daughter,
Margaret

Letter XIII

Date of writing unknown (possibly 1866)
Published 17 July 1868 in Y Tyst Cymreig

Dear Parents

I have had the most dreadful dream, which has had a great effect on my mind, and I hope that you will not be annoyed with me for sharing it with you.

I dreamt that I was standing on a rotting plank which was suspended between earth and heaven. Jesus had led me there. I shouted towards heaven for someone to help me, but no one responded and I feared that I would lose my footing and fall. I knew that if I fell from that height, I would be in tatters by the time I reached the bottom. But whilst in this precarious situation, I saw my Redeemer coming towards me, smiling gracefully. But as He came closer, His appearance changed and He started to look sad and merciful and I feared that if He said something, it would probably be troubling words. When He reached me, He asked was I there yet? I replied, 'Yes, Lord'. 'Oh', He said, 'you're not one of the children, otherwise someone would have come to fetch you from there, a while ago.'

Oh dear parents, where was I to go? If I had thrown myself headlong down off the plank, my soul would still be the same. If only He had been willing to let me throw myself into His wonderful arms, where I would always be safe. But that wasn't the way it was meant to be. My cup was yet far from being filled.

I then remember walking through heaven. But I could not see much that was heavenly about it. There was an earthen floor with a few chairs and some thirty-five to forty women kneeling quietly, with some sort of cloth thrown over their heads. I went past these and down some steps to a large but unpleasant room which was so dark that I could barely see where I was going. When I lifted my eyes I saw my greatest

Judge, the just and holy God – the one who is unable to look upon the bad. What light there was in the room emanated from Him and, as the Psalmist says, 'Clouds and darkness are round about Him; righteousness and justice are the foundation of His throne. A fire goeth before Him, and burneth up His adversaries round about.'[27]

As soon as I looked at Him, I saw wrath and resentment in His countenance. When He looked at me, it nearly overpowered me to the ground. He did not say a word to me for a moment and, in that painful time whilst I was standing mute in front of Him, I felt the most intense heat coming up the side of my face. Then I looked in that direction and, woe me, I saw that I was on the edge of hell. There was a morbid odour emanating from there, and roaring noises, such that I could barely hear the echo. The place was of enormous proportions, with a small door in the middle which was never opened unless a sinner was being thrown in.

Little had my composure and mind recovered when I felt the same unseen power again forcing me to look into His face – a face that I would have given the world to be annulled from its presence (if such words are appropriate). I had to stay there without anyone to speak on my behalf. Where was my Saviour now? The one whom I had trusted my soul to, for such a long time. As soon as I raised my head, with my eyes heavy with tears, the awful sentence passed over me. My Judge said to me, shaking his head and throwing his arms indignantly, 'Go away from me, you are worse than the devil'.

Dear parents, this was such woe, this was distress, anguish and an aching soul. I find it difficult to find language strong enough to illustrate how I felt, as no soul can go through such an amount of wretchedness without some sort of feeble hope, but I felt that I had no hope at all. However, I did not obey my destiny, but threw myself at His feet, crying, 'Mercy, mercy'. Then I remembered that it was too late and said, 'If only I could see my Intercessor, I could say in truth and spirit that the sight of Him would make me sing in this very deep river'.

As I was still continuing to cry for mercy, having disheartened to such an extent that I was despising my life, I tried to obey my destiny and endure being thrown into the eternal fire. I raised my eyes to look for someone to intercede on my behalf. I did not have the pain of searching for too long before I saw someone coming. Dear parents, it was no one less than my blessed Saviour. He said something quietly to his Father (and yes, *my* Father by now), and that changed His appearance, and He looked so merciful and compassionate, as David says in Psalm 103, verse 13: 'Like as a father hath compassion on his children, so hath the Lord compassion upon them that fear Him.'

By now tiredness and tribulation had eaten deeply into my heart. By then I could not appreciate the glory of heaven. This was what I had longed for, for so long. The only sin bothering my conscience was the fact that I had accepted blessedness in my life and that I had not done anything in the name of the Lord to deserve it. I thought that it was my idleness in doing His work which had been the reason for my perdition.

When I rose to my feet, I looked down to the earth and saw three women sitting with arms crossed, speaking to each other. When I saw how unconcerned and unaffected they were, I shouted until the place where I stood began to shake; my voice was like thunder tearing through the clouds. 'Work for the Lord before it is too late', I shouted. But they took no notice and, as I worked out how to make the women listen to me and take note, I awoke.

I cried all day, and the following day and my mistress cried with me. I pray that my nightmare will not portray reality.

From your daughter,
Margaret

Letter XIV

Written in early 1867
Published 28 August 1868 in Y Tyst Cymreig

Dear Parents

I received your letter on 10 December and its contents brought surprise and joy to me, because I had not thought that you would have another baby. The water from the river Jordan will therefore be useful, and I would like to know what Mr Rees, the preacher, thought of the water.

I shall continue with my description of Jerusalem since I have not been anywhere to give you news. Near the market hall is a road which leads to Joppa Gate or the western gate and that road goes to Bethlehem, Hebron, Gaza and Joppa. This gate is known in Arabic as *Bab al-Khalil*. It is about five yards in height, at a width of four yards and is made of iron. A soldier stands guard there night and day. All of Jerusalem's gates were built in the year 1542 by the Emperor Suleiman. You can walk along the city walls quite easily as Jerusalem is a small city compared to the cities of Europe.

There are only four gates into the city at present. The northern gate is known in Arabic as *Bab el Sham* and in English as Damascus Gate. The roads from here go to Damascus, Nablus and the northern countries. The eastern gate is known as St Stephen's Gate (in Arabic *Bab Sitti Maryam*), and leads to the Garden of Gethsemane, the Mount of Olives, Bethania, the river Jordan and the Dead Sea. The southern gate is known as Zion Gate (*Bab Sahyun* in Arabic) – nearby is the grave of David. Beyond this gate is the village of Siloam and the mountains of Moab can be seen from here. Jerusalem lies 2,000 feet above sea level, but the mountains of Moab are another 700 feet higher.

Now that I have described the outside of the city, I shall finish describing the interior. You can buy just about anything in the *souks* of the city. But the whole place is totally higgledy-piggledy. In one little shop, there is a sign above it which says that the following are for sale there: 'Bibles and Frying Pans'. I think that it is a rather improper and indecent activity to sell both of those items together. The best way I can describe these little shops is by comparing them to the open-fronted forges back home, which shoe horses. The trader sits cross-legged outside his shop, like a tailor. At the other end of the shop there will be a bottle with a large 'belly' full of bubbling water, boiling away. Attached to this bottle will be a four- to five-yard pipe. There is a piece of ivory at the stopper end of the pipe and the trader puts this in his mouth and, from time to time, he draws from it, as if smoking. Everyone, men, women and children smoke in this fashion in this country, as soon as their lungs have developed enough to inhale. You will even see some Europeans who have been here a while smoking in this fashion.

The best road in Jerusalem is known as the Christian Road. I walk along this road quite often, deep in thought with spiritual matters, yet wary of tripping over on the jagged edges. But even if I were to trip over, I am sure that the Holy Spirit would help me along and let me carry on with my journey. Most of this road is sheltered by a covered area, which makes the road rather dark and slippery underfoot. However, you soon come out of the sheltered part and into the bright light, which encourages you to go forward. Many of the city's barbers live on this road and they work in front of their homes – so people have their hair trimmed or shaved in the open air for all the world to see. The barbers are quite rough in the way they treat their customers. When they wash heads, they shake the gentleman's head so vigorously until it clicks. The barber and customer are often covered in sweat by the end of the procedure.

Not too far away from here is the grave of the Lord. More

people walk in this area than in any other area of Jerusalem. Nearby is a tall column where the Turks shout at the top of their voices each morning, evening and midday *'Alah al acbar la il Alah sidna Mahomed alica i Salam a Mahomed il resal Alah'*, which means 'In the morning it is better to pray than to sleep, come to pray to God, there is no other God but Him, and Mohammed is His prophet'. This is heard at four o'clock every morning.

I must close now, hoping that you are all as well as I am here.

From your dear daughter,
Margaret

Letter XV

Written 3 March 1867
Published 9/16 October 1868 in Y Tyst Cymreig

Dear Parents

I was very happy, as usual, to receive your kind letter and the cards. I have to say that I was a bit surprised when I saw the photograph of my brother John. He has put on a great deal of weight since the last photograph I saw of him. I am also rather disappointed with him because he has not made the effort to spare half an hour in half a year to write a letter to me.

Now for some news. Since last month we have been living under a shadow in Jerusalem, as the Sultan has ordered the Turks to kill all Christians who live there. But, a month earlier, in January, all was well, as it was the holy month for the Muslims and if a Muslim harms anyone during that month, he or she is seen to have committed an eternal sin. We were even allowed to go out without lanterns (but if we had done this in any other month, the Turks would have taken us off to prison). During January, the Muslims are not allowed to eat, drink or smoke during the day. You can hear cannon fire at six in the morning and at six in the evening, which is the signal to Muslims that they are not allowed to eat between those hours. When all the fasting was over, they had a feast which lasted from Tuesday until Thursday. But once the feast and the holy month were past, word spread around Jerusalem that the Turks would come and try to kill us at midnight on the Thursday. We thought that this story was false until we heard what had happened in Damascus five or six years ago, when very many children were left as orphans.

At about half past nine on the Thursday night we heard gunshot, which was very unusual and that made us very fearful and panicked, and everybody started praying. Our prayers were answered, as nothing in particular happened that night. However, someone said that the danger would not be over until May. So, my dear parents, keep praying for us.

I was very saddened to hear of the death of the son of Rev. R Thomas, Hanover, who you tell me has been killed in China.[28] This young man went to China full of hope and was murdered soon after he arrived. He died for a very good cause, which I am sure God is grateful for. Dear parents, I would be more than happy to die for the cause.

I shall now finish my description of Jerusalem. The city is divided into four quarters – not that there is any visible physical division, but there are different nationalities living in each quarter. The Christians live in the western quarter, the Turks in the northern quarter, the Jews in the eastern quarter, and the Armenians in the southern quarter.

I went to the Jewish quarter last week. Their houses (or maybe more correctly, their cabins, because that is what they remind me of) look quite wretched. They have no doors and the doorway is the only source of light into the home. They have uneven earthen floors and the houses are evidently damp and unhealthy. Most Jews are poor and pitiful.

We went to visit the Wailing Wall, which is not far from an old fort. Some of the stones in the Wailing Wall were enormous, some four yards by two yards each, and look similar to marble. There was a hole in the corner of the wall (as part of it is the old temple of Solomon), which led to the holiest sanctuary. The Jews are of the opinion that this is the only place where God will listen to them, and so they pray to God, Abraham, Isaac and Jacob at this place, to help them be restored to their old country and holy city. If you listened to some of them you would think that their hearts were about to break.

If only I could speak Hebrew and tell them of the new Jerusalem, and of the new Lord who is ready to accept them, the Messiah, Jesus Christ. But then I thought, what a shameful thought of mine – who was I to say such a thing – all I could do was pray for them. Whilst we were at the wall, there were dozens of Jews there, most with copies of the Old Testament and the Talmud (which is the explanation of the Old Testament), in their hands. Some of the Jewish women could not read, therefore an old man with long, white hair sat opposite, reading to them.

There were a few Turks about the place also and they were mocking the Jews. And, as the Turks left, one of the old Jewish ladies started to shout at them, and then when I looked at her a few minutes later, her clothes were alight. The Turks had set her on fire. But the flames were extinguished quickly. I was shocked to see the 'old Lords of the land' reduced in such a way under the feet of pagans.

I must end now. Hoping that you are all well and comfortable,

Margaret

Letter XVI
Written April 1867
Published 30 October 1868 in Y Tyst Cymreig

My dear parents

I have just had the pleasure of seeing two gentlemen from Caernarfon and they have offered to take something back to Wales for me. Therefore I am sending a bottle of water from the river Jordan for the baptism of my mother's next child. But if my mother has no further children, then the water can be used to baptise the first grandchild. The water will keep pure for a number of years, but it would not be wise to open it until necessary.

I have not had much time to prepare presents, as I only met these two gentlemen on the Sunday morning just gone, and they are to leave Jerusalem on Wednesday morning. Therefore, I have only had this Tuesday afternoon to prepare, as Monday was tied up with the washing.

It was my master who saw the two Welshmen first, and he mentioned to them that he had a maid who would give a pound to hear someone say 'bara chaws' [bread and cheese]. The master had told them that these were the only two words that he knew in the Welsh language.

Well, I have to close now, hoping that you are all well, as I am. Do send a letter when you receive the gifts.

From your dear daughter,
Margaret

Letter XVII
Written 3 May 1867
Published 28 December 1867 in Y Tyst Cymreig

Dear Parents

I am very sorry if my previous letter [*sic*] has caused so much concern at home. I do not think there is much to worry about in Jerusalem at the moment. Since I last wrote the leaders of the Protestants here have been considering developments, and they decided to go and visit the Pasha, the president of the city, to ask him to protect the Christians. The Pasha has signed a piece of paper ensuring that he will do so, but I think he signs it begrudgingly. I now feel perfectly safe here, because I believe in my God and, if the worst came to the worst, I am sure that He will help us find a way to escape, much as He helped Lot to escape from Sodom.[29] I think you will probably have had a visit from the family of the bishop[30] by the time you get this letter, and they should have put your minds at ease.

I have been on a short visit to Artas, which was once known as the Gardens of Solomon. It lies some six miles from Jerusalem. I had a holiday, so eight of my friends accompanied me there. I was fortunate enough to be able to borrow my mistress's donkey, but that turned out to be particularly stubborn that day, so I exchanged it for a friend's mule, which was supposed to be a little calmer. But a mule is a mule, whichever country you are in, and this particular mule was very difficult. I was soon abandoned by most of my friends' more responsive animals. A companion, who was walking, kept me company. About half way there, a man jumped out on us. He was ugly, half naked, with the few clothes that he had on him, tattered to pieces. His skin was nearly black due to the sun and he was holding a knife in his hand. My companion was frightened witless, but I thought little of it. As the man approached us, I started to speak to him in Arabic (I can now speak the language rather well). The ugly man looked at me strangely when I said to him, 'Peace to you, sir' and responded by shouting 'Your mule won't move'. So I replied, 'There are people following us'. Then he shouted, 'Give me *backshish*'. I looked at him a little more fiercely and calmly said, 'Go in peace, I do not even have one *paras* (which is one-twentieth of a penny)'. At that point, my mule seemed startled by something and jolted off. When it eventually stopped, I asked my friend if she had stuck a pin in the back of the mule. She said she had not, but when we looked at the back side of the mule, there was some blood running from a small wound.

We caught up with our friends eventually and arrived in Artas some two hours later. We visited three lakes which are known as Solomon's Lakes. The lower pool was very beautiful, with a well-worn staircase going down to it. But there was hardly any water in the pool.

We got lost on the way back to Jerusalem. So everyone had to dismount and walk, but not quite walk either, but slide their way down the hills because they were so steep. By the time we got to the bottom we were delighted to see some lunch laid on for us by the parents of one of my friends: roast lamb, green peas and boiled wheat. These are a family of returning Jews, and they have suffered greatly as a result. The wife had left her parents, brothers and sisters when very young for the God who has done so much for her.[31]

I have no more to write about this little visit. I hope that you do not tire of what I write. I have to finish now. Send my warmest wishes to people in the chapel.

Your dearest daughter,

Margaret

PS: I am delighted to hear that my brother John has joined God's people. My warmest wishes go to him.

Letter XVIII
Written 2 July 1867
Published 18 January 1868 in Y Tyst Cymreig

Dear Parents

I received your letter of thanks and I am pleased that my gifts have given such pleasure to so many.

I am feeling rather lonely at the moment, because two of the girls have left Jerusalem and have gone to school in Beirut. They will not be returning home for another fifteen months. I had become so very fond of them and it is difficult to be apart from them. There were many tears when they left for Beirut, with the girls saying, 'Oh Jones, if only you came with us, we would be perfectly happy'. I send the two letters that the youngest has written to me for you to see. The letter the eldest wrote was too heavy to send. They write to me as often as they do to their parents.

I received a letter two days ago from my brother Thomas,[32] complementing you on your kindness when he came to visit you. He told me that he had joined the Baptists. He said it was a natural thing for him to do, as he lived in a house full of Baptists. If that is what his conscience told him, then I cannot find any fault with that. I hope that he does not take the sacrament of baptism as the basis for his salvation. He says that he will not, and if he really is a true Christian, then I am glad that he has joined God's people somewhere with any sect of Christians.

I have been spending my evenings sleeping in the sanctorum with twenty children, being those that I keep evening Sunday school for. I have been teaching them many Welsh tunes, but with English words, of course. When the children see me coming towards them, they always rush to greet me.

My health seems to be faring better than at any time since I arrived in Jerusalem – due mostly to the pleasanter

Bethlehem Chapel, Rhosllannerchrugog, at the end of the nineteenth century (by permission of the trustees of Bethlehem Chapel)

Bethlehem Chapel today

Rev. Elias Frankel,
Margaret's employer
(Conrad Schick Library,
Jerusalem)

Christ Church, Jerusalem *c.*1860s (Conrad Schick Library, Jerusalem)

Christ Church,
Jerusalem today

The altar of Christ
Church (Stacy Klodz)

Christ Church, Jerusalem today

Some of the sites visited by Margaret in Jerusalem and Bethlehem:

Al-Aqsa mosque in Jerusalem's old city (Eric Rufa)

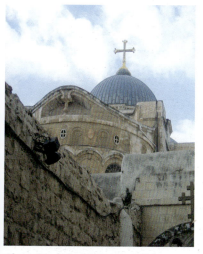

Church of the Holy Sepulchre, Jerusalem (Eric Rufa)

The place where it is thought Jesus Christ died, inside the Church of the Holy Sepulchre (Eric Rufa)

The Garden of Gethsemane (Eric Rufa)

Via Dolorosa,
one of the main
thoroughfares in
Jerusalem (Stacy
Klodz)

Mount of Olives (Eric Rufa)

The graves of Jews on the Mount of Olives (Stacy Klodz)

Jews praying at the Western Wall (Stacy Klodz)

Bethlehem skyline (Stacy Klodz)

Manger Square, Bethlehem

LLYTHYRAU CYMRAES YN NGHANAAN.

LLYTHYR VII.

Anwyl Rieni,—Yr ydwyf wedi cael y breuddwyd mwyaf ofnadwy, ac y mae wedi cael effaith mawr ar fy meddwl; ac fe al'ai na fyddwch yn ddig wrthyf am i mi ei ysgrifenu.

Breuddwydiais fy mod yn sefyll ar ryw fath o ystyllen wedi hanner braenu. Yr oedd wedi ei gosod i fynu rhwng y ddaiar a'r nefoedd. Yr Iesu a fy arweiniodd i yno, ac yno y bum yn gwaeddi tua'r nef am i rywun ddyfod i'm cynnorthwyo yn mhellach, ond y cwbl yn ofer, ac yr oeddwn yn disgwyl mai colli fy ngafael a syrthio y buaswn. Yr oeddwn yn gwybod os disgynwn o'r fath uchelder mai yn chwilfriw y buaswn cyn cyrhaedd y gwaelod. Tra yn y sefyllfa yma, bron wedi rhoddi pob gobaith i fynu o fod yn gadwedig, yn gorph ac enaid, gwelais fy Mhrynwr yn dyfod tuag ataf dan wenu yn siriol a graslawn; ond fel yr oedd yn nesu tuag ataf newidiodd ei wedd, ac aeth i edrych mor drist a thosturiol arnaf fel yr ofnais iddo ddyweyd gair, rhag mai o'r drwg y byddai; ond pan gyrhaeddodd ataf, gofynodd ai yno yr oeddwn i eto? Atebais inau, 'Ie, Arglwydd.' 'Ah,' ebe fe, 'nid wyt ti yn un o'r plant, onide buasai rhywun wedi dod i dy gyrchu oddiyna er's llawer o amser.' O! fy anwyl rieni, i ba le yr oeddwn i fyn'd! Pe buaswn yn taflu fy hun yn bendramwnwgl i lawr, yr un fuasai fy enaid o hyd. Oh! na fuasai yn caniatau i mi daflu fy hun i'w freichiau bendigedig, lle y buaswn byth yn ddyogel; ond nid felly yr oedd i fod—nid oedd fy nghwpan eto ond pell oddiwrth fod yn llawn.

Y lle cyntaf yr wyf yn cofio fy hun wedi hyny yw yn cerdded drwy'r nefoedd; ond nid oeddwn i yn gweled dim nefoedd o honi. Llawr pridd oedd iddi, ac ychydig o gadeiriau, ac o 35 i 40 o ferched a rhyw ddilledyn wedi ei daflu dros eu penau, a'u peniloedd ar eu gliniau, ac yn bur ddistaw; ond aethum heibio i'r rhai hyn, ac i lawr un gris i ryw ystafell eang arall, ond pur annifyr, ac mor dywyll nes prin yr oeddwn yn gweled pa fath le oedd, a pheth oedd yno; ond pan godais fy llygaid i fynu, canfyddais lygaid fy Mharnwr Mawr, a'r Duw cyfiawn, santaidd hwnw, yr hwn nas gall edrych ar ddrwg, a hyny o oleuni oedd yn y lle; o hono Ef yr oedd yn tarddu, a hyny ond ychydig iawn, fel ag y dywed y Psalmydd,—Cymylau a thywyllwch sydd o'i amgylch ef; cyfiawnder a barn yw trigfa ei orseddfainc ef. Tân a â allan o'i flaen ef, ac a lysg ei elynion o'i amgylch.' Cyn gynted ag yr edrychais arno, gwelais lid a digllymedd ofnadwy yn ei wedd; a phan edrychodd arnaf, yr oedd y faith nerth yn ei olwg nes bron a fy llethu i'r llawr. Ni ddywedodd Efe un gair wrthyf am ryw enyd fechan, ac yn yr ychydig amser poenus hwn, tra yr oeddwn yn sefyll yn fud o'i flaen, teimlais wres angherddol yn dyfod i fynu at ochr fy wyneb. Yna edrychais i'r cyfeiriad hwnw; ond Och fi! gwelais fy mod ar fin uffern. Yr oedd yno arogl afiachus a'u dyrchafu oddiyno, a swn rhuadau fel yn mhell iawn, fel nas gallaswn ond prin glywed yr adsain (echo). Hefyd yr oedd maint y lle yn anferthol, ac o amgylch ei dop, wedi ei blastro a chlai, ond un twll bychan ar y canol, a chauad ar hwnw, ac nid oedd byth yn agored ond tra byddai pechadur yn cael ei daflu i mewn.

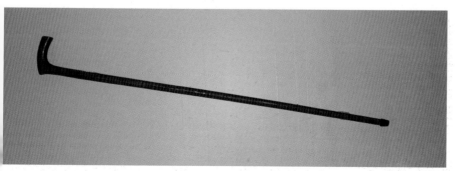

One of Margaret's letters published in *Y Tyst Cymreig*

The walking stick which Margaret sent to her father from Jerusalem in September 1867 (Gwynne Williams)

Three photographs of Margaret taken by John Thomas *c.*1875 (by permission of the National Library of Wales)

Mizpeh, Mogador (19th century) where Margaret worked as a teacher and missionary amongst the Jews (Conrad Schick Library, Jerusalem)

MOROCCO,

A'R

HYN A WELAIS YNO:

GAN

"Y GYMRAES O GANAAN.'

WREXHAM :
ARGRAFFWYD GAN HUGHES AND SON, 56, HOPE STREET.

Titlepage of the volume *Morocco, a'r hyn a welais yno* (by permission of the National Library of Wales)

Central Congregational Church, Ipswich: Margaret was employed as a Bible woman here (photograph from *Ipswich Congregational Church: Jubilee 1853–1903*)

The cover and the first page of Margaret's diary, 'Miss Jones' Lady Visitor's Diary', from her time working at Central Congregational Church, Ipswich (John Oxley Library, State Library of Queensland)

> Ipswich Queensland
> — 1889 —
>
> Diary of religious work. by Margaret Jones
>
> Commencing Wednesday April 3rd
>
> Calling as directed with Miss Berry & Mrs Perkins I found them too busy to come and introduce me to the people the morning is an awkward time for visiting
>
> Visited one house where I found a German housewife who told me she & her husband were members of a Baptist Church, expressed an opinion that there was plenty of work for me in the neighbourhood. The next called upon was a sick nurse named Mrs R. she acknowledged to have neglected religion for years both in private & public, however she was very

Mary Anne Jones (1869–1953),
Margaret's half-sister
(Bronwen Hall)

Mary Anne and her husband,
William Parry. They were
married in Ipswich, Queensland,
on 8 July 1891 (Bronwen Hall)

Eden Station, the home of James Josey (*Queensland Times*)

James Josey, Margaret's husband
(John Oxley Library, State Library of
Queensland, Neg: 178969)

The grave of Margaret Josey,
the Welsh Lady from Canaan
(Bronwen Hall)

weather. Another reason is that there is not as much general malaise, famine, or locusts in the city this year as compared to years gone by.

I am going to tell you about how Jewish babies are treated. As soon as they are born the babies are bound with a bandage, from the neck to the ankle, and are unable to move their arms at all. They are not washed for months, other than behind the ears and armpits. In the house the baby is hung from the ceiling in a sort of hammock and rocked backwards and forwards when someone passes by. When going outdoors, the baby is placed in a sort of sling.

I am unsure if I told you this before, but husbands will not get to see their wives-to-be until the day of the wedding. Parents and nearest relatives do the matchmaking, although one would have thought that those to be betrothed would try to see one another on the sly. My friend from the hospital, the matron, told me that one of her servants was to be married before too long, to a girl of twelve years. The twelve-year-old girl was very upset when she happened to come across the sight of her husband-to-be one day before the wedding.

After the wedding the married couple must stay together for the next twenty-four hours. But after that, they can be strangers for seven days. All Arab girls oil their faces with muslin rags and then put a cloth over that.

I must close now. Best wishes to you all.

I am your dear daughter,

Margaret

Letter XIX

Written 22 September 1867
Published 1 February and 13 November 1868 in
Y Tyst Cymreig

Dear Parents

I received your kind letter and the newspaper about two weeks ago and I fear that you will be very cross with me for not replying sooner. I have got many excuses that I could offer but, after consideration, I realise that none of them are good enough. So you must make do without an excuse at all.

I am sending you some gifts with my very best wishes. There is a four-page booklet for you to keep, some locusts too, if you wish to keep those, and I would like you to give the other flowers and the wings of the locusts to any relative or friend who wants to receive them.

My dear father, I do hope that you get good health, and a long and comfortable life to enjoy the walking stick.[33] The bottom half of the stick has come from the river Jordan. I hope people will not be as envious of it as they were of the water from the river Jordan that I sent you earlier. I also hope that the neighbours will not think it as being Catholic or foolish of you to use the stick – I shall be pretty sorry if they do. The knob of the stick has been made from wood from the Mount of Olives.

I have read your account of the excellent and interesting Sunday school meetings in Rhos and, as I said at the time, I only wish that there were something similar here in Jerusalem, but there I go, grumbling again. However, I am not really complaining as we are a very happy band of worshippers here on Mount Zion. There are about ninety to a hundred worshippers here. Do not laugh – I know that that is quite small compared to the congregations of the chapels in Rhos.

There are three classes of members in the church although, to be honest, all men and women should be equal, but not here in Jerusalem it seems. The highest class includes the bishop, parsons, missionaries and their families. The next class down or the second class (of which I am a member) is the merchants, bankers and shopkeepers. The lowest or third class are the poor people. But dear parents, do not think for one moment that I am proud of not being counted amongst the poor. It is true that I think little of the poor people of Jerusalem, at least some of them, not because they are poor, but because they are so lazy – to an extent that *I* have never seen before. The truth is, and the poor admit to this also, the reason that they are lazy is because of the climate and the heat. I know that it is difficult to cope with the weather at times, but it is just a difficulty, not an impossibility. A Welsh person would certainly put up with it. The Welsh people work through all kinds of weather to keep their families, and lean on no one other than themselves. No, a Welshman would not starve himself and the family just because they felt delicate in the sun. The poor are also as proud as they are lazy, and they would rather see their children starve than go and find some food for them or let them become servants and maids. They say that being in service has no meaning in life, but I have always been proud to be in service.

Now I want to tell you of the situation of the family. The master is a returned Jew and when he had to leave his home, he left a father and mother, five brothers and two sisters without a hope of ever seeing them again. But, this did not stop him from praying for them. He has prayed for them for the last twenty years and his prayers have been answered, as his youngest brother has recently been converted to Christianity. Georg Frankel is twenty-four years old; he is a bit fat, but eats very little. He is also quite quiet and never asks for anything. He was a soldier in Poland.

My master and mistress have gone to Beirut to visit two of their children, and have been away for the last three weeks.

So that means that I am queen of the place! I now have my own servant and he is very faithful in doing everything I ask of him, because my mistress told him from the beginning that I was his mistress from now on, and that he should respect that. I also have a mule, which is just as obedient as the servant. I go out with the youngest daughter every day, whilst Georg keeps house.

The family of the bishop have gone to visit Wales sooner than I thought. Mrs Gobat has promised to bring a bundle of items back to me, so I am also sending you four pounds, if you would be so kind as to buy the items on the enclosed list for me and give them to Mrs Gobat.

I must end now, in the hope that you are all healthy and comfortable. I have been a little unwell and quite lame now for about a month, but thanks to the compassionate Lord, I am getting better slowly.

I am your dear daughter,

Margaret

Letter XX

Written 22 November 1867
Published 8 February 1868 in Y Tyst Cymreig

Dear Parents

I was sorry that my delay in writing to you had caused you some uneasiness, but I am glad you told me, otherwise I would have been guilty of the same sin this time again. I had thought of delaying writing a little longer, because I was awaiting the return of Bishop Gobat and his family from their travels in the next three weeks. I am so looking forward to his return – I was intending that this letter would be an opportunity for me to thank everyone for their kindness, but as you would rather get a letter sooner rather than later, you will just have to make do with this dry, dull letter.

I was delighted to hear that Thomas Jones, the joiner, had turned his back on the devil and embraced Jesus Christ. If only thousands more would follow his example, so that Satan could grind his teeth at the loss of so many followers, making him retreat into his lair and break his heart, and give up his work of bestowing damnation on souls as a bad job.

I was surprised and saddened by the deaths of the Rev. John Phillips, Bangor[34] and David Roberts, Manchester. Do remember me fondly to Mr Lettsome – I rejoice with them at the birth of a son. I have a bottle of water from the river Jordan in my chest, but I will need to work out how to get it to him.

Since I last wrote I have visited one of the largest Jewish synagogues and have seen how they celebrate the Festival of the Tents.[35] I visited the synagogue with Mr and Mrs Hursteim, who are the master and mistress of the hospital. We left home at five in the afternoon and travelled through the Jewish quarter of the city where all the shops were closed and everybody was dressed to the nines. The ladies were all wearing red, purple, or yellow clothes with gold thread running through the garments. (These clothes are handed down from one generation to the next, as well as jewellery such as bracelets, necklaces and head adornments.) The petticoats of many of the men were also purple. The Jews adorn their homes both inside and outside with green branches and palm leaves for this occasion.

Firstly, we went to the main synagogue, but we were late in arriving and the service was already over. This synagogue is the most attractive building in Jerusalem, with lamps of pure gold showing the place where they keep the five books of Moses. The windows and walls are ornate, with many musical instruments, such as harps and cornets painted onto the walls. But it seems that the only musical instrument that the Jews play these days is some sort of large nut, which has been cut in half; it is spoken of in Isaiah 24:8–9.

Then we visited another synagogue, where soldiers

guarded the door and were most threatening when we intimated that we wished to enter the building. However Mr Hursteim knew the chief rabbi and sent word to him and entry into the synagogue was granted. There were very many Jews inside and we had to push our way through the horde to get near the front. I fell over several times on my way to finding a window sill to sit on. From there I had a good view of the crowd. I have to note that many Jews seem to have pale, grey faces, much like the Lord himself.

There was a pulpit in the middle of the synagogue, where the rabbis and the important people of the city stood or sat. Everyone else stood on the floor surrounding the pulpit and, with so little space, everyone stood shoulder to shoulder or back to back, because the seating had been turned upside down. The rabbi, dressed in white, called for silence and then shouted loudly that whomsoever offered the most money would be allowed to take Moses's five books out of the cupboard. The sum of ten shillings was rejected for this honour and, after much banter, the scrolls were eventually taken out and placed in the arms of ten boys. Then, hats and items of clothing were thrown in good humour at the rabbi, with all eyes on him to see which offerings he would choose to wear. He chose a fur coat and a large hat. The rabbi was then carried on the shoulders of two of the strongest men in the building. He was lifted and thrown up and down, which made my heart beat faster just by looking at him. The Jews call this dancing; if you look at 2 Samuel 6:14 there is an explanation.

Then a procession was formed with the rabbi at the head, followed by the ten boys carrying the scrolls of Moses, and then by most of the congregation. The retinue was a loud affair with much clapping of hands, shouting and playing of the nut-like instrument which I described earlier. Everyone looked as though they were thoroughly enjoying themselves, especially the rabbi. The ladies, however, had to observe the whole scene through the windows. They are usually allowed into the gallery of the synagogue, but not on this occasion, because the service is too long.

As we left the synagogue, in the midst of all the merriment, the rabbi hit one of the gold lamps with his hat and spilt all the oil on the best clothes of one of his assistants. The assistant was greatly displeased and both of them started to fight, quite forgetting the fact that they were still inside the synagogue. We went home once the fight was over.

I am delighted to say that we have had some butter this week, the first for seven months. You have no idea what it is like to have to go without bread and butter for a whole seven months. The weather is still very warm, with no need for fires – the doors are still kept wide open during the day. Rain is uncommon – it rained for two to three hours about a fortnight ago. As I said a while ago, it rarely rains in Jerusalem and they hardly ever have any storms of thunder and lightning either. But when a mid-winter storm does arrive, it is quite terrifying and worse than anything that I have seen in Wales.

The Pasha, the governor of the city, has recently rounded up all the city's beggars, prisoners, widowed men without children, and all strong orphaned boys to build a road that will go at last throughout Assyria. All the male outcasts of society have been assembled to move the large rocks to make this road. There is little doubt in my mind that the words of the prophet in Isaiah 62:10 are coming true. The Jews seem to think that when the road is completed the Messiah will come. And if He does not come, the Jews will think that He is already here. Oh, and to return to the men who are making the road, their wages are as much bread as they can eat and as much water as they can drink.

Well, I must close now. I hope that you forgive me for all the errors in this letter. Do remember me to all my religious brothers and sisters and all my friends in Rhos.

This, from your affectionate daughter,

Margaret

Letter XXI
Written c.March/April 1868
Published 4/11 September 1868 in Y Tyst Cymreig

Dear Parents

It was so kind of you to send me a photograph of Mr Rowlands, the minister. I hope that God will bless his ministry and gain him many souls from the claws of Satan to the bosom of Jesus Christ. Do remember me kindly to him and his wife Mrs Rowlands. I am glad that she liked the little cross I sent her.

Since I wrote to you last, I have had the pleasure of seeing five Welshmen: two from Liverpool (one of them, David Jones, was the master of my cousin, Daniel Phillips), Thomas Lewis from Bangor, a Mr Parry, also from Bangor, and a Mr Roberts. The five gentlemen had met my master and mistress at the bishop's house, and Mr Roberts had told my mistress the most extraordinary story. The previous evening, he had taken out a pair of new shoes that his wife had packed for him (but had not needed on the journey to date), and the shoes had been wrapped in newspaper. That newspaper was *Y Tyst Cymreig*, and Mr Roberts was astonished to find one of my letters to you written on that piece of newspaper. That particular letter had referred to the Frankel daughters entering school in Beirut.[36] I was surprised therefore to read from your letter that four of my letters had already been published in the newspaper. I would appreciate it if you could send me copies, as I have forgotten much of what I wrote about.

I do not have any accounts of travels in this letter because I have not been anywhere. And although Joppa Gate is but two to three hundred yards from our house, I have not seen it this year as I am fearful of walking needlessly because I get rather lame these days.

However, I thought I would give you more details of how

the locals live their lives here instead. Girls from as young as six years walk around in what I would describe as a bed sheet, yet they go to bed in something that I would call a gown. Like many English girls, they wear both together on occasions, with a gown of crinoline on top as well. I shall let you imagine what that might look like. But I am sure that some young children would think that they look like ghosts.

Men go to bed fully dressed and they even take their tarbushes – their red caps – with them to bed. They do not have an all-over-wash but two or three times a year. But they wash their neck and ears once a week. Even if they are completely filthy, there is no law in the land nor any authority which can make them wash their face more often than once a week.

We had a male servant in the house a while ago, and when my mistress saw how dirty he was and that he did not have a single shirt, she offered him one of my master's old shirts on the proviso that he would wash his ears and neck. But all the determined servant did was to say that he would take the shirt now, but wash at the end of the week, as usual. And, as the servant had already seized the shirt from the mistress, she let the matter be. But lo and behold, the next morning, the servant was to be seen parading around the local market with the new shirt on top of all his other rags for clothes, with a large F (for Frankel) informing everyone of where the shirt had come from.

No man will tolerate his wife kissing him but on the hand, and this is something which she must do each time the husband returns to the household. A man will not show any signs of affection towards his wife in public either. Once, an Arab lady visited the household of some missionaries, and at the end of her visit she asked the lady of the house if European men generally behaved in that fashion towards their wives. When told that that was the case, the Arab lady replied that she wished that she'd been raised in a Christian country, where women were treated as creatures that possess souls, and not as creatures of the fields.

I have to admit that I do not write my letters all in one sitting, but as and when I have some leisure time. I know I told you that I had not been anywhere, but I have just received an invitation from the parson and his family to go to visit the Mosque of Omar, which is the current place of worship of the Mohammedans. The mosque is built on the foundations of the old temple of Solomon. I have been longing to see this place which was once so very holy, for the last three years.

I have now had the chance to visit the holiest place in the world, as described by Jehovah in 1 Kings 9:3 – do read this for a flavour of my visit. Today, a sixty-foot wall surrounds a marble platform which is 1,500 feet long by 1,000 feet wide. There are six entrances onto this platform and, without doubt, this is the most beautiful place in Jerusalem. Surrounding the platform is one of the most fertile pieces of ground in the city. It is a shame that practically naked and dirty children and their parents, sitting around doing little, distracts from the view of the lovely green grass. However, the leaders of the Mohammedan faith are much more holy than their counterparts in the Christian faith, because when they are deemed holy enough to live within the temple, they are not known by their first names alone, but as Saint Abraham or Saint Mohammed, and this is because they have seen the grave of the prophet Mohammed and have been to Mecca.

We were asked to take off our shoes before walking onto the platform. We were then led into the mosque, which is a large circular building. We saw some beautiful stained glass windows, a ceiling made of bronze, and intricately carved railings made of wood surrounded the interior of the building. But there was nowhere to sit, and a multitude of doors led away to other parts of the compound.

There was a wire door next to the altar and the Muslims place pieces of thread around the wire if they need help to have children or some other important matter. There were also pieces of wool and cotton rags on the wire in the windows, and this did make the place look like a rag shop. In a room under the altar (which is also on Mount Moriah), is the spot where Solomon used to tie up his mare, the place where Abraham sat, where David prayed and Elijah rested, and many other superstitions regarding Mohammed happened. But there is little mention about what Jesus did there, apart from one place where there is an oblong stone, which some say was his cradle.

The Muslim sheik told us about his prophet and, as he did so, I kept on staring at the place where I thought that Jesus might have sat in the middle of all the scholars, teaching them in a way that no man had ever taught others. There was something so sweet about this image in my mind, whilst listening to the noise of the worshippers of another prophet.

We were led to several other buildings. One of them was very old and below ground. The stones in the wall were enormous – easily five to six yards in length and two yards wide. Some of the stonework had started to break off, so I scraped at it and took some shards home with me as a memento. I will send some of it to you in a letter. There were some bridges between one building and the next and a fountain too, but these could not have been there when the temple was in its glory.

Many pillars stood very close to each another in one of the buildings. The sheik informed us that if you were able to squeeze between these pillars, then you would reach heaven. For those of us who were a little plumper, there were some further columns, a little wider apart. But if you were very fat, and could not squeeze through any of those columns either, it was assumed that you must have been very wicked anyway, and that you would never get entry to the blessed eternity.

As we left we were shown the grave of Solomon. We made our exit from the mosque through the gate next to Lake Bethesda. And I could not help but have visions of Jesus walking along those very same footpaths.

I have no space to write anymore. Forgive me for all my clumsy comments. Remember me kindly to everyone at chapel, especially my old friend Edward Phillips.

This, from your dearest daughter,

  Margaret

Letter XXII
Written 10 July 1868
Published 25 December 1868 in Y Tyst Cymreig

Dear Parents

I received your letter three days ago. I was sorry to hear that you had been so worried about me. You need not be concerned – if only you knew how many friends I have, and how kind they are, as only the best of friends and relatives can be. But more than that do remember that I live under the wing of the Lord.

Now I shall tell you all my news or at least all that has happened since I last wrote to you. I am writing this letter from a hospital kept by women called the Prussian Protestant Sisters of Charity. I have already been here for five weeks and I have endured more pain in my body in the last three weeks than in the whole of my life put together. I have been bedridden for the last three weeks and I cannot bear for anyone else to try to move me either. You can hear my screams over half of Jerusalem. But thanks be to God that the worst of the pain has virtually left me by now.

I hope that I can endure being moved in two to three days

time as my bed needs to be repaired. The bed is not made of feathers and is no longer soft and comfortable at all after three weeks of lying here. The doctor who is treating me is the kindest, gentlest and most noble man I have ever met, and he has told me that the reason for the pain in my knee is because it has been bound too tightly in the past. As a result, that binding has stopped the flow of blood and that has resulted in the sinews and tendons of my leg deadening. This had been done by one of the other doctors. But this doctor is new, and he comes from Germany.

But now my knee has been released from its very tight bandages and my tendons have enlivened, but they are still a little inflamed. The doctor thinks that my knee will get better and that I will be able to walk reasonably well, but I may be quite stiff. I really do hope that I get to walk again, but I fear that that may take quite a while.

The doctor comes to see me twice a day and, if my knee is very sore at night, he gives me something similar to the water gun that the boys of Rhos play with, but that this gun is a proper one made of silver and glass. He fills it with something similar to water, but he calls it opium. He pushes the opium into my leg and, after it has been injected, I am perfectly fine. I do not worry about sitting up or lying down either. I often tell the doctor that this opium is the best treasure in the land. You see, if it were not for that, I would have to wash my eyes with cold water all night to keep myself awake, because if I fall asleep I tend to move around and that can be very painful.

But, that is enough about my troubles. Let me tell you about the place where I stay. The hospital is full of Arabs, but I am quite fortunate in that I have a room of my own. It is a small room but has two windows, a table and chair, a chest of drawers, as well as the bed.

Every single one of my friends in Jerusalem has been to visit me. My mistress either visits daily or sends something good for me to eat. When the pain in my knee actually started, my mistress very nearly lost her mind and with eyes full of tears said, 'Oh, I should not have let you come in here. Let me carry you from here, Jones, and take you back to your bed at home. I'll send some men to carry you home. Do not let them kill you in this place.' But I replied, 'My mistress, I cannot bear anyone coming anywhere near me.' And her response to that was, 'Well hurry up and get better then, and I will look after you at home. I would do anything for you, if you would only come home. Do not let them kill you in this place.' She really does think that the doctors are at fault for my condition and that they are trying to kill me. But she is happier now, as I seem to be getting better.

But my mistress is having a bad time of it in other ways too because my master has been travelling around Canaan for the past six weeks. One night, he was robbed of everything that he owned as he slept in his tent. He has not managed to find the culprits. However, the master is to return to Jerusalem from Beirut with his children and one of their teachers in the next two days. And here am I, lying in bed unable to do anything to help out. Many of the missionaries and their wives have visited me each week. The two youngest daughters of Bishop Gobat come and sit with me for a few hours. Everybody is very kind and they bring me good food too. So there is nothing for you to worry about.

I cannot remember if I told you about the two Misses Gobat whom you met in Wales. The eldest has married and has stayed with her new husband in London. The other will go to Germany, as she is to marry there within the year. So all in all, their trip to Europe has been very successful.

I am, dear parents, your dearest daughter,

Margaret

Letter XXIII
Written 2 September 1868
Published 8 January 1869 in Y Tyst Cymreig

Dear Parents

I received your letter a few minutes ago, and had virtually given up all hope of receiving word from you. I note from the postmark that the letter had been a month on its journey. As the post leaves here soon, I do not have much time to write a reply, but I think that that would be better than waiting another fortnight for a letter from me. I do not have much cheerful news I am afraid, as I am is still in my hospital bed, and getting better slowly but surely.

I get up out of bed about once a week so that the bed can be made. I am not in too much pain, but I still cannot walk, not even with crutches. But there is nothing I can do but hope and pray to the Lord for a full recovery, if that is His will.

Please do not stop praying for me, as it is the prayers of the faithful that heal the sick, and it is the Lord who raises us and, if we do sin, He will forgive us. And, as not one jot of the Lord's words is wasted, I adhere to his promises. Indeed I feel better that the Lord has seen fit to rebuke me in this way and cleanse me for eternal happiness, instead of letting me wallow in my sins. I say from the bottom of my heart that blessed be His holy name.

I have been laid up on my hospital bed now for twelve weeks since last Monday gone. After being here about a month, the doctor put four folds of starched bandages on my leg, from my toe to above the knee. But my leg became so painful that the following day the doctor had to remove all the bandages. He was not happy, and of the opinion that this was all far too soon for any good to have been done to my knee. I did have the most awful pain in my knee afterwards, and I suppose that the doctor's opinion was probably correct.

My leg is now hovering in something like a child's sling and is surrounded by wool. But dear parents, do not think for one moment that I am breaking my heart or crying about it, in fact, I am as cheerful as a bird in a bush. But if you do continue to fret and worry about me, you will soon discover that you will get tired of doing that too and it can be quite unpleasant. I do, however, worry that you may start to think that I will believe, as an Englishman would, 'What will be, will be. What cannot be cured must be endured, and the more cheerful it is endured, the better in the end.' I belong to those who think that 'if it happens, it happens', because I think that that is the best way to deal with it.

My master has been to visit, and he brought with him a looking glass for me and placed it on the wall opposite the bed so that I could watch everybody passing on the road in front of my hospital window. One day, I saw something that I had never seen before – the face of a dead man who had thirteen wives. He was a sheik and had been to all the Muslim holy places. When he returned home from his pilgrimages, one suspicious wife suspected that he loved one of his other wives more than her, and judged that her husband did not deserve to live any longer, and that it was her duty to put an end to his life. She therefore placed poison in his food. As soon as he realised what was going on, he despised all his wives and his children, and made his way to hospital, but he died the following day. He said that he was going to go to heaven and that the only persons he wished to meet there were one of the sisters from the hospital and a servant who had attended him before he died. He did not want to hear from any of his relatives at all and, in that turbulent frame of mind, he died. I saw him carried out of the hospital on a plank, with his bare face looking towards heaven and a narrow strap across his eyes.

It seems that I am unable to write short letters, whether or not I am in a rush.

I am, dear parents, your dearest daughter,
Margaret

Letter XXIV

Written from Beirut, 22 October 1868
Published 15 January 1869 in Y Tyst Cymreig

Beirut

Dear Parents

You will see that I have left my dearest Jerusalem. I departed the city on the 24th of September and was carried on a bed to Joppa. The pain was unbearable at times, especially along the narrow footpaths over the mountains when those people carrying me could not but shake the bed. When I arrived in Beirut, I was greeted by Mrs Thompson[37] in the kindest way; if I had been her daughter, she would not have treated me any better.

As soon as I was comfortable, she sent for two of the best doctors in Beirut. When they arrived they looked at my knee, shook their heads and said that the doctors in Jerusalem had done a great deal of harm to my knee – not on purpose of course – but through a lack of knowledge. The Beirut doctors said that I would not be able to get out of bed for another six months at least, and that I should not break my heart if I was not able to get up out of bed for another year. We shall see what God's will shall be.

However, I am now able to sit up and do some sewing for a few hours each day. The doctors have advised me that I need to eat the best possible food and drink a great deal of wine. So you see, some poor man will need to work for two days just in order to keep me for a day! I am most grateful that circumstances have led me to this place. I feel quite at home here, because I think it was the Lord's kindness which delivered me here. The doctors have, however, advised me that I might need to seek medical attention in England, because the doctors there are perceived to be more intelligent.

I have been pleading with my doctors here to change my leg for a cork one, because I am yet but very young. I cannot foresee this leg carrying me for another sixty years. I think that it would be far better for me to have my leg cut off, because it is of no use to me as it is. But they will not cut it off because, if they did, it would put my life in danger in this hot country. If it is their honesty which makes them speak in this way towards me, then it is of great credit to them. I just hope I get better sometime.

I shall tell you a little about the house where I am staying in Beirut. Most of the rooms in the house are as large as the Methodist chapel in Ponkey. I am not sure how many rooms there are in the house altogether, but the children have promised to carry me to see the other floors of the house one day. The children have already started to carry me on a sort of a sofa with railings (on which I was carried from Jerusalem) around the garden. These people are very kind to me and have taken great trouble over my well-being. I hope that the Lord will bless and reward them.

Mrs Thompson is the daughter of General Lloyd, who lived in Wrexham for years. Mrs Thompson's grandmother spoke excellent Welsh, although Mrs Thompson herself speaks no word of Welsh. She has made me write a long letter to her sister, who is a very rich lady, to inform her about all the problems that I am suffering from because of my knee. I do not know what Mrs Thompson's sister will make of the letter. I am not used to writing to such important people.

My dear father, I do wish that you would write me a line or two more often. I was so very saddened to hear that so many family members are unwell; I hope that they are getting better.

I left Jerusalem on a Saturday morning, with the most wonderful lady that I have ever met. She is the daughter of a noblewoman from Germany and her father is a baronet. But she is no more proud than if she had been raised in a mountain hut. Miss Sack looked after me ever so well on my journey to Beirut, and never let me out of her sight for one moment. And, when I was in real pain, she would give me medicine. If I had been the baroness and Miss Sack the maid, she could not have been more helpful to me. Miss Sack was a first-rate doctor and could turn her hand to do virtually anything, from educate a princess to teach a cook how to make food and clean a kitchen. She does all those things herself anyway on a daily basis. And on top of all her accomplishments, Miss Sack is also very godly and that is the most beautiful thing about her. She also preaches and has been known to preach to up to a hundred people in this house. Miss Sack would find all this praise rather embarrassing – she certainly would not show off about it.

I am your dearest daughter,

Margaret

PS: When Miss Sack and I left Jerusalem on the Saturday, we saw a sick man on the road and gave him a lift in our cart. He was very grateful. Mr Frankel and the children came to meet us at Joppa on Tuesday and stayed long enough for me to rest before continuing my journey to Beirut. Mr Frankel said that a parcel had arrived for me from Wales. The children jumped up and down when they saw that the parcel contained red and white buttons, cough lozenges and all sorts of sweets. The parcel had been sent by my cousin, Daniel Phillips, and had been handed to my master five minutes before leaving Jerusalem. Do thank him kindly for it.

PART IV

The Length and Breadth of Wales

The 'Welsh Lady from Canaan' intends to visit parts of Wales on the following dates: Bangor 31 October, Llandderfel 10 November, Bala 11 November, Rhuthun 14 November...

(*Y Tyst Cymreig*, 28 October 1870)

Margaret returned from Beirut to Liverpool on a waterbed in January 1869. She faced treatment on her knee, followed by recuperation which could take months, if not years. On her return home she felt rather distressed and depressed. After all, she'd had to rely on the help of comparative strangers in Beirut, people such as Mrs Bowen-Thompson and her friends, and if it hadn't been for them, who knows what could have happened to her. Elias Frankel had not paid a single penny towards getting his sick servant home for treatment, and Margaret certainly felt resentful about this.[1]

Once disembarked, Margaret went to the home of eminent surgeon Dr H O Thomas[2] at 49 Kent Street, Liverpool. Treatment commenced soon after and Margaret then made steady improvement at the home of her parents in Rhosllannerchrugog. And it was there, in Rhos, that Margaret realised that she had returned to the country of her birth as somewhat of a celebrity.

Margaret's last letter from Canaan had been published in *Y Tyst Cymreig* in January 1869. It had already been suggested that the letters could be collected together and published as a book. Margaret's father had expressed the idea in a letter as early as the spring of 1865, when Margaret had only been in Canaan for a matter of months (Margaret's response can be seen in a letter published in Y Tyst Cymreig on 31 July 1868). At the time, Margaret feared that her letters weren't interesting enough to be published, but hoped that if they were collected in book form, that her readers would forgive her errors. She was adamant that she would only allow a book to be published if it were deemed that it would do some good.

But it seemed that publishing the letters in a book would do Margaret a great deal of good. She was penniless. The small amount of money which she had earned in Jerusalem working for the Frankel family had gone to pay for doctors and medical attention on her knee in the Middle East. It appears that the Frankel family had contributed very little to the costs of treatment there either. The doctors had done very little for her in Palestine, and she had to raise funds to pay for treatment in Liverpool. So, she had to take advantage of her new-found popularity, and publish the letters in a book.

Letters of support for the publication of a volume began to appear in Y Tyst Cymreig in January 1869. Gwilym Hiraethog (the Rev. William Rees, 1802–83) was the author of one of them and his letter was published four times that month.[3] Gwilym Hiraethog was one of the most popular and famous orators in Wales at the time and he was a minister with the Congregational Church in Liverpool, a newspaper editor, and a poet. He wrote in his letter of support that many had written books about their travels to Canaan, but he was of the opinion that Margaret Jones's letters from that part of the world were far more interesting than the others. He called her a talented girl, with a good eye for detail.

A second letter of support came from the Rev. T Ll Jones (1831–79), a minister with the Congregational Church in Machen, Monmouthshire, and it appeared in Y Tyst Cymreig on 15 January. He urged everybody to buy the book. A week later, an update about Margaret's health appeared in the same newspaper. It mentioned that she was now residing in Liverpool with her surgeon, who had himself been unwell recently. Now better, he was confident that he could give Margaret his full attention and he was also sure that he would not need to break her knee for it to heal. It was also noted that she was very keen to return to Jerusalem as soon as she was fit again, because that was where her heart lay.[4]

She was certainly the subject of many newspaper column inches on her return to Wales. Another intriguing aspect to her story was discussed in a letter to *Y Tyst Cymreig* on 29 January. J Rowlands, from Rhosllannerchrugog, was responding to the rumour circulating that Margaret wasn't the true author of the letters which had appeared in *Y Tyst Cymreig*. J Rowlands assures readers that he has seen and read the letters in Margaret's own handwriting, and that they were exactly as they had appeared in the newspaper. Undoubtedly, there were plenty of people around who were envious of Margaret's success and wanting to do their best to belittle her. J Rowlands chides those who questioned the authenticity of the letters. And with his daughter laid up in bed, not knowing if she'd ever walk again, that was not the only dark cloud on the horizon for her father, Owen Jones. J Rowlands adds that the family are also in mourning for two of their children, who were buried in the same grave on the same day in January 1869.[5]

It is worth speculating why so many rumours arose as to whether Margaret was the genuine author of the letters. She admitted herself that she had only received a few weeks of schooling in Rhosllannerchrugog. Undoubtedly, she was self-taught in much of what she knew. However, she spent much of her childhood amongst the religious community of Bethlehem Chapel in Rhos, with people who were interested in the arts, who read their Bibles, who wrote poetry, who bought newspapers. Through this cultural immersion she would have gained a good standard of spoken and written Welsh. Margaret was not only a brave young woman, but she was clever too. She had the ability to learn languages with ease. Her English had been good enough to be employed by the Frankel family at the age of twenty; she spent two years living in Paris and learnt French, and in her letters from Jerusalem, she notes her ability to communicate in Arabic.

In his letter J Rowlands implored the local distributors of *Y Tyst Cymreig* in England and Wales to keep a list of people who were willing to buy *Llythyrau Cymraes o Wlad Canaan*. Her father, Owen Jones, was also a distributor of *Y Tyst Cymreig* and it was this network of people which ensured that the book sold as well as it did. The first of Owen Jones's advertisements was placed in the newspaper on 29 January 1869, stating that he was collecting the names of subscribers who were willing to buy the book.

This was how books were sold in those days, not only in Wales but throughout the world. Another book published in 1869 about the travels of an author in Canaan (in 1867) was *The Innocents Abroad* by Mark Twain (Samuel Langhorne Clemens, 1835–1910). Twain's book had also started out as a series of letters to newspapers in New York City and San Francisco before being collected in book form. It sold well as a result of canvassing agents roaming the country seeking subscriptions before it was published. And those willing to put their name down for the book saw it as signing up to create 'durable items of cultural furniture'.[6] The same was true of Welsh books. Regular readers saw it as their cultural obligation to support new authors, especially those who had a religious message to sell. But, as in the United States, there were occasions when books of little literary merit were also supported, and many may have thought privately that *Llythyrau Cymraes o Wlad Canaan* was in this category.

The distributors of *Y Tyst Cymreig* got to work promoting Margaret's forthcoming book. It was printed in early March

1869 and was on sale for sixpence a copy. By mid March, 700 people in the Rhos area alone had already purchased it.[7] The book was advertised weekly in *Y Tyst Cymreig* for a number of months. By June, in response to a letter in the newspaper from Brochwel inquiring after Margaret's health, her father Owen responds by saying that only 200 copies from the first print run remain, and that there are discussions about printing a second edition, which would include some extra information and illustrations.

Not all of the 24 letters published in *Y Tyst Cymreig* were included in the book. The book contained only 17 of her letters, with some heavily edited. The 'Foreword' was written by Dr John Thomas (1821–92), Liverpool, a prominent minister in the Congregational Church (and a great uncle of the dramatist Saunders Lewis). There were letters of commendation from Gwilym Hiraethog, Thomas Lewis from Bangor (who had met Margaret in Jerusalem in 1867) and David Jones from Liverpool (who met Margaret in Jerusalem in 1868). The letters were not dated in the book, but most had been in *Y Tyst Cymreig*.

As a result of the publicity in *Y Tyst Cymreig*, congregations of Welsh women, in particular, marvelled at Margaret's bravery and ability, and bought copies of the book in their droves. Seven print runs of the book were arranged, although it is uncertain how many books were in each print run.[8] The book was printed at the offices of *Y Tyst Cymreig* in Liverpool. Margaret's first venture in publishing had been a resounding success. And, just as in this day and age, in order to create more publicity for the book, Margaret started to travel, but instead of making the rounds at the TV and radio stations as is done today, Margaret did the equivalent of her day – she became a travelling lecturer across Wales.

2

Margaret was very fortunate that she had a lecture topic which would be of interest to congregations all over Wales. Not only would she be able to describe biblical sites to her audiences, but she would also be able to refer authoritatively about Canaan, and this was of particular interest to the Welsh at this time. In the middle of the nineteenth century many influential Welshman, such as Michael D Jones (1822–98) and John Mills (1812–73), discussed the possibility of establishing Welsh-speaking colonies in remote parts of the world. Michael D Jones, who had been ordained a minister with the Congregational Church in Cincinnati, Ohio, felt that the Welsh people who had emigrated to the United States had been americanised very quickly and had lost much of their Welsh traditions, and so he became a fervent advocate of establishing a Welsh colony in Patagonia.[9] In the mid 1850s, a minister with the Calvinistic Methodists, the Rev. John Mills, who was also a well-regarded musician and had worked as a missionary with the Jews in London, suggested establishing a Welsh colony in Palestine,[10] and this a few years before the Welsh colony was eventually established in Patagonia in Argentina in 1865. Although there was a good deal of discussion in the press, especially in publications such as *Y Drysorfa* [The Treasury], *Yr Amserau* [The Times] and *Y Faner* [The Banner] between 1856 and 1858, little came of the idea of establishing a colony in Palestine, because many opposed the suggestion. So it seems that Margaret's Welsh audiences had another reason to be interested in her lecture about Canaan, as day-to-day life there was of interest to them also.

As Margaret began to lecture in various parts of the country, she was joining the ranks of a large group of people who spent their lives in this fashion. Listening to a travelling lecturer was an important part of the Welsh social scene at that time. There had been a number of religious revivals during the nineteenth century, in particular the 1859 revival. These revivals were responsible for engendering a thirst for knowledge. As one commentator succinctly remarked, 'an enlightened heart and an empty head do not go together'.[11] Worshippers strove to improve themselves; they would read any books that they could get hold of and would faithfully attend the lectures of speakers who visited the chapel. The chapels were the social centres of Welsh villages and towns by the mid nineteenth century. Most social activity revolved around them, be it a concert, a drama, choir practice or evening class, and a variety of activities were held each week. The public lecture became very popular in the chapels at this time, and would generate income for the chapel as well as the lecturers. Dozens of men, predominantly, were seen travelling the country, with one or two tested lectures up their sleeves. Many of these lecturers spoke about their religious experiences, and it is surprising how many had travelled to Canaan and were now ready to share their observations with others.

Many Welsh towns started following the example of English towns in establishing 'mutual improvement societies'. The two-hour lecture became the mainstay of those societies. Such were the numbers of would-be lecturers at one time in Wales that a correspondent of Y Cylchgrawn [The Magazine] complained that the numbers of people lecturing was a plague on the land. One of the most popular orators of the time was Gwilym Hiraethog, a Calvinistic Methodist who became a minister with the Congregational Church.[12] His beliefs were controversial; not only did he support female authors such as Margaret, but he also advocated radical causes such as nationalist organisations in Europe. He presented these ideas to audiences all over Wales.[13] Some believed that he was the 'father' of the popular lecture; he delivered his first lecture on 25 November 1846 at the Concert Hall, Lord Nelson Street, Liverpool. His subject was William Williams, Pantycelyn, the famous Welsh hymnist, and a large audience of Liverpool Welsh came to listen to him.[14] He would also address audiences on varying topics, such as astronomy and geology.

By 1850 the chapels of the Congregationalists and other Nonconformists would add the popular lecture to their weekly schedules and this continued until the end of the century and beyond. But as the popularity of the lecture grew, questions were raised suggesting that secularism was entering chapel life through the back door. Were people attending chapel for faith and religious reasons, or were they visiting chapels for entertainment and socializing purposes?

These questions did not deter the rapid increase in the numbers of lecturers on the circuit. Another famous Welsh lecturer was the Rev. Thomas Levi (1825–1916). He not only shared his ideas from the pulpit, but also in the thirty or more books that he wrote on religious themes.[15] Other Welsh lecturers of note were: Thomas Penry Evans (1839–88), an exceptionally popular preacher, who had a homely style and would lecture on topics such as 'Being a man' and 'Being honest'; John (Gomer) Lewis (1844–1914) from Swansea, who lectured on subjects such as 'The World Fair' and 'Abraham Lincoln', several thousand times apparently; William Jones (1834–95) from Fishguard, who would travel the country speaking about 'John Bunyan' and 'Charles Dickens'; John Rhys Morgan (1822–1900), a Baptist minister from Llanelli, who had in excess of thirty subjects in his repertoire, and Benjamin Thomas (1836–93), who travelled the land sharing his experiences about his 1860 trip to the United States.[16]

3

There were a few women who travelled the country sharing their experiences too. One particular lady was Sarah Jane Rees (1839–1916) who was also known by the poetic name Cranogwen. She was a contemporary of Margaret Jones, and both ladies met once at one of Margaret's lectures. Cranogwen was a very famous lady in Wales; she had achieved a great deal and was well respected in her day, but she had not achieved the *one* thing that Margaret had experienced, which was a visit to Canaan.

Cranogwen's story is a fascinating one too. During her lifetime she was a sea captain, a poet, a musician, a preacher, a temperance movement leader, a school mistress and the editor of a Welsh women's magazine. She'd been sent away by her mother at the age of fifteen to learn to be a seamstress. She hated the work so much that she ran away to sea, and enjoyed life as a sailor for two years. In time she would gain her master of the seas certificate. At 21 years of age, she decided to live on dry land for a while. She took charge of the school in her local village, Pontgarreg, near Llangrannog. She was headmistress for six years, before succumbing to itchy feet once more. She was a promising public speaker, and so she joined the expanding popular lecture circuit and started visiting chapels around Wales. She travelled the land for three years, lecturing and preaching on subjects such as 'Wales, her religion and education', 'Money and Time', 'The Home', 'Things that go wrong' and the female Welsh hymnist 'Ann Griffiths'. Cranogwen became more and more well known the length and breadth of the country, and one rather envious poet quipped that she was the 'two sovereign, difficult Goddess'.[17] Cranogwen was paid two sovereigns for each of her lectures. It seems that the male poet wished to ridicule her popularity. She was yet to turn 30 years of age.

And to celebrate that birthday, she went on a voyage to the United States in 1869. There she spent several months lecturing to Welsh audiences in states bordering New York City. She then ventured west to the Rocky Mountains. This was not an easy journey to undertake; it would have been even more fraught for a foreign lady travelling on her own.

Margaret Jones, therefore, had a female trailblazer working the popular lecture circuit ahead of her in Wales. But, the life of the female public speaker was not an easy one, as Cranogwen's case exemplifies. There were very many men, like the poet quoted earlier, who vehemently objected to seeing a woman sharing her ideas with a large group of people in a public place. And these objectors were quite vocal in their displeasure.

Many were of the opinion that women should not do any public work whatsoever. They could not think of a situation arising where there was a need for a woman to speak from the pulpit. They quoted the Bible to support their arguments. And one opponent even went as far as saying that the world had come to an end when he saw Cranogwen lecturing from the pulpit![18] Others, just as uncharitably and cruelly, said that Cranogwen didn't belong to the one gender or the other. Indeed, it was many of those male fellow lecturers on the circuit with Cranogwen that encouraged such ideas.[19] They were envious of her popularity, as hundreds of people would attend her lectures. They resented the fact that so many chapels requested Cranogwen to come to speak to them and that their engagements became fewer as a result. It appears that Cranogwen had the ability to make men of stature cry, as happened when she spoke at a gathering in Merthyr Tudfil. She had such an effect on the chairman of the evening, the local Member of Parliament, Charles Herbert James, that he was unable to thank her at the end of her lecture for her efforts.

In an article in *Y Drysorfa* magazine in 1866, Thomas Levi tried to defend Cranogwen and women like her. He suggested that those who were opposed to female lecturers should read the stories of Deborah in the Bible. He was of the opinion that it was the fairer sex which ruled the world by now, and cited Queen Victoria as an example. Levi had read many books written by women, and had sung many hymns and poems composed by women. The final point in his argument was that if whatever on offer was universally good, then it did not matter if it had come from the hand or mouth of a woman or a man. Interestingly, Thomas Levi was a well-respected travelling lecturer himself. But his stance did not stop those who argued against women lecturers travelling around the country. Many responded to the *Drysorfa* article by saying that women such as Cranogwen had left the circle into which they had been created by their Maker. Many derogatory poems were published, one in particular by Gelyn Athrod, from Myddfai, Carmarthenshire, in *Y Cylchgrawn* highlighting Cranogwen's lifestyle. Cranogwen and her fellow female lecturers' reaction to all this fuss was to carry on as before.

Most of these travelling lecturers were not only working for personal financial reward, but also to raise money for a local cause. The audience were charged at the entrance to each lecture. The lecturer would then be paid a fee and the remaining monies would be set aside for a charity (in the case of Margaret Jones, the Palestine Missionary Fund) or towards the building of a new chapel. The profits made at a popular lecture or drama contributed a great deal to the cost of erecting many Nonconformist chapels in Wales in the nineteenth century.

4

Margaret's knee was on the mend. Her book was selling well and she had also started to sell some photographs of famous places in Canaan. From mid March 1870, an advertisement appeared in *Y Tyst Cymreig* stating that the book continued to be on sale for sixpence and that it could be bought directly from the author herself now, from her address at 32 Windsor Street, Liverpool.[20] She was also selling photographs of Joppa Gate, Main Road Jerusalem, the Wailing Wall, Hezekiah Lake, the Garden of Gethsemane, The Holy Grave, the site of the Old Temple and of the Welsh Lady from Canaan dressed as one of the women of Bethlehem, for sixpence each. It is unknown as to how Margaret got hold of so many photographs to sell. She may have brought some photographic plates home with her from Jerusalem and had copies of them made in Liverpool.

Possibly photographer John Thomas (1838–1905) had assisted her with the task of selling photographs of herself and views of Canaan. Thomas had been raised in Cellan, Cardiganshire, and was apprenticed as a draper in Lampeter before working in a clothes shop in Liverpool. He was forced, due to ill-health, to seek work out of doors and he travelled the country working as a salesman selling writing paper and photographs. John Thomas realised how few photographs of famous Welsh people he had to sell. He bought a camera in 1863 and invited a number of famous Welsh preachers to sit for a photograph. He established the Cambrian Gallery in Liverpool in 1867.[21]

His photographs from the nineteenth century are now kept at the National Library of Wales in Aberystwyth and amongst them are three portraits of Margaret; she wears traditional Middle Eastern dress in two photographs, and the fancy gown of a Western lady in the third. An accompanying note with each photograph says 'Y Gymraes o Ganaan, Miss

Jones Vocalist', and it is thought that the photographs were taken around 1875, which suggests that these were not the photographs of herself sold in *Y Tyst Cymreig* in 1870.

The book continued to do well. Margaret's popularity, especially amongst the readers of *Y Tyst Cymreig*, encouraged her to do more to spread her message. On the evening of Tuesday, 5 July 1870, she gave a lecture in her native area, Rhosllannerchrugog. She was amongst friends, trialling out her lecture for the first time in the family chapel, Bethlehem, the Congregational chapel in Hall Street. If she was going to get a warm welcome anywhere, then this would be the place. And despite feeling very nervous, she stood on her feet for two hours. Ten days later, her efforts as a lecturer were reviewed in *Y Tyst Cymreig*. The correspondent, JG, described the event in great detail. He said that she had kept the interest of the audience throughout the two hours very well; the audience had been of the opinion that she had come through the ordeal brilliantly. All the pictures which she painted were very lively; she'd used verses from the Bible wisely. In fact, he described the use of these biblical verses as being 'golden apples in a work of carved silver'.[22] Margaret had also mentioned the work of the mission in Canaan, and had spent quite some time speaking about the schools of Mrs Elizabeth Bowen-Thompson, a Welsh lady from Flintshire. She told her audience that Mrs Bowen-Thompson had been particularly kind to her in Beirut. But there was far more to this talented lady than just being a good Samaritan.

Elizabeth Maria Bowen-Thompson (née Lloyd; 1812 or 1813–1869) had been appalled by the civil war between the Druze and Maronite Christians in 1860: ten thousand Christians were slaughtered by the Druze in a massacre in the Lebanese hills. In 1867, Mrs Bowen-Thompson arrived in Syria and Lebanon and set about establishing schools for the widows and orphans left by the civil war. She founded many schools, but her work came to an abrupt end in 1869 (a few months after Margaret had left Beirut), when she unexpectedly died. Margaret revealed in her lecture that the work of Mrs Bowen-Thompson had left quite an impression on her and that her dearest wish was to return to the Middle East as soon as possible to help continue the wonderful work that Mrs Bowen-Thompson had started.[23] Margaret, it seems, was more impressed with Mrs Bowen-Thompson's efforts in the Middle East than with Elias Frankel's work. Three years after her death, the volume *The Daughters of Syria* (1872), a narrative of Mrs Bowen-Thompson's efforts to evangelise Syrian families was published.[24]

Margaret must have breathed a huge sigh of relief at the end of her first lecture. She was delighted with the comments about her performance in the newspaper, the publication which had staunchly supported her since returning from Canaan. Some six weeks later, she was ready to give another lecture, but in front an unfamiliar audience this time. What kind of reception would she get? She need not have worried.

Another of *Y Tyst Cymreig*'s correspondents, Ap R, was just as effusive in his praise. The content of the second lecture, held in Mold on 22 August, was similar to that of the first. Interestingly, one of Margaret's first comments was to say that she wasn't a keen supporter of seeing so many women speaking in public, but she felt that she was justified in doing so as she was also raising funds to send evangelical information to the 'unenlightened residents of Canaan'.[25] Ap R commented that many people had suggested to him that going to listen to her lecture would not be any different from reading her book. Ap R sought to dismiss this, saying that her lecture would have been beneficial to him, either way. Miss Jones was the third female lecturer to have graced the dais of this particular chapel. Margaret was following the in footsteps of Miss Evans (Mabws) who regarded herself as a professional lecturer, and Miss Rees (Cranogwen) who had a strong mind and, in his opinion, was the Welsh Eliza Cook.

Miss Jones did not regard herself as a lecturer, he said, and it had never occurred to her to ask for a fee for her lecture. But the correspondent Ap R could assure the readers that Miss Jones 'failed on the best side'. She had a sonorous and trenchant voice, plenty of good language which was easily understood, and a huge treasury of memorised biblical verses. Very many were pleased with her performance and Ap R saw some of the poorest members of the congregation putting money in the collection box at the end.

Two further lectures were held close to home in September. Having heard her at Queen's Street Chapel, Wrexham on Friday evening, 16 September, *Y Tyst Cymreig's* correspondent, Gwynfro, was of the opinion that Miss Jones was as good an orator as she was an author.[26] And in the same edition of *Y Tyst Cymreig*, JP mentioned that a large audience had come to see her after tea at Brynsion, Brymbo the following Monday.

A week later, Margaret travelled westwards, to unfamiliar territory, the slate mining area of Bethesda, Caernarfonshire. She would deliver her lecture three times in a week at various Congregational chapels. *Y Tyst Cymreig's* correspondent, Gyfylchwr, was the first to comment that the lecture was very amusing. Despite the lecture being mostly educational and beneficial, he had been surprised to hear a lady give such a witty account of events.[27] Gyfylchwr had attended four lectures on Canaan in his time, and Miss Jones's was by far the best. He felt that the reason for this was the fact that Miss Jones had actually spent time in Canaan, something which the other three, apparently, had not!

The audience were reeling with laughter as Margaret told stories of the bakehouse and the lazy servant Maria. According to the correspondent, her evident decency made her warm to her congregation instantaneously. She was the most unaffected lady that he'd ever seen; everything about her was likeable and attractive. High praise indeed. Gyfylchwr also notes that 2,000 copies of Margaret's book had been bought in the Bethesda area already. Finally, he implores congregations throughout Wales to insist on being able to hear her lecture.

Gyfylchwr was evidently quite taken by the young Miss Jones. And by then Margaret was feeling quietly confident about her abilities as a public speaker. At the end of October, an advertisement appeared in *Y Tyst Cymreig* noting that the 'Welsh Lady from Canaan' was about to start a journey around north Wales. She would be undertaking lecturing engagements, starting in Bangor on 24 October and finishing in Bontnewydd near Caernarfon on 12 December.[28] Some weeks, she would be delivering her lecture on five occasions. She would be on the road for nearly two months at the end of 1870.

Margaret's fame was increasing by the week. And as she travelled from village to village during those months, there was no shortage of families who were ready to open their doors and welcome her to stay overnight with them. It was quite a scoop to have Margaret Jones as a guest at the breakfast table. And Margaret's audiences were growing by the week. In Dwygyfylchi, on a Friday night in late October 1870, she had to speak at Pen-y-cae, the Calvinistic Methodist chapel, because Horeb, the Congregational chapel, was far too small to accommodate the audience. The correspondent Meini Hirion's effervescent account of the evening speaks of Canaan being a country where milk and honey flow, and the same could be said of Miss Jones, who has the 'milk' to make her lecture interesting. It appears, from his report, that Margaret was accompanied by another lady. This lady would dress up in the clothes of a woman from Bethlehem, and this visual display helped get Margaret's message across. Margaret also commentated about the superstitions of the residents of Canaan, which may have seemed quite strange to a religious congregation in Wales.[29]

In Bangor on 24 October, 3/6 was charged for an entrance ticket to her lecture. A profit of £10 was made that night. In

Bala on 11 November, the chapel was overflowing according to the correspondent, Cyfaill. In Port Dinorwic on Friday, 18 November, a £20 profit was made; the pews of Moriah Chapel had never had so many people sitting on them. The correspondent there summed up by saying, 'the Welsh lady has keen eyes, an enlightened head, a tender heart, a clear voice and a lithe tongue. She managed to rivet the attention of the crowd for the two hours that she stood on her feet.'[30]

In Pwllheli on 1 December, the Member of Parliament, Love Jones-Parry came to listen to her; he called her language 'pretty and attractive'.[31] And, according to the correspondent Josephus, Margaret had been the guest of some of the most respected families in Caernarfonshire over the previous few weeks. In Bontnewydd on 12 December, a substantial crowd turned out to see her despite the most dreadful weather.[32]

Within a few weeks, Margaret had become the talk of rural, religious north Wales. By the end of December she thoroughly deserved a rest. But Margaret was already planning further tours for 1871.

5

The first reports of Margaret's visits to more southerly areas of Wales came when she lectured in Tal-y-bont in Cardiganshire. The weather was poor on the night of 17 January, and it was evident that the buzz created by Margaret in north Wales had not filtered south, as only a few came to listen to her.[33]

This may have been quite a surprise and a disappointment for Margaret, as there are no further reports of her lecturing in this area at a later date. In February she was back in more familiar territory, in Caernarfonshire, visiting several chapels in Ffestiniog, Maentwrog and Trawsfynydd. In Dolwyddelan, in early February, the correspondent commentated that she had spoken for two hours and that every single eye and ear had been glued to the lips of Miss Jones.[34] And Margaret was beginning to feel a little more confident now about prospective locations to deliver her lecture. *Y Tyst a'r Dydd* [The Witness and the Day] (*Y Tyst Cymreig* was renamed in January 1871) noted that she had two lecturing commitments over the border in England, in Liverpool on 28 February and then in Hanley, Staffordshire, on 1 March. Margaret attracted a huge congregation to the chapel in Grove Street, Liverpool, despite there being two other Welsh lectures scheduled in the city that night. In Hanley it was necessary to borrow another chapel for the evening to accommodate the crowd. By the beginning of March, Margaret had already raised £200 for the mission fund.[35] She would lecture at the Tabernacle, Shrewsbury in March before travelling to the south-east of England.

On the evening of the 1871 census, 3 April, Margaret was a visitor at the home of a Navy captain, John Newby, and his wife Mary, who was born in Wales. Although no newspaper reports have come to light to prove that Margaret had delivered her lecture in the Welsh chapels of London, the fact that she was a visitor in a Welsh home in Rotherhithe, Surrey, suggests that an invitation to lecture had come from the large Welsh-speaking community in London and the surrounding area.

Bethesda, the Congregational chapel in the coal-mining town of Merthyr Tudfil was her first lecturing engagement in south Wales, on 18 May. She then moved on to Pontardawe, and lectured in the Methodist chapel, before speaking in chapels in the Swansea area. By the end of June, she was heading north, and held a lecture at Llanwrda and Llanwrtyd Wells. Then she returned to the valleys of south Wales. At Carmel Chapel in Treherbert in the Rhondda valley, it was estimated that 700 people were present, an astonishing number considering that the coal miners were on strike at the time.[36] Amongst the congregation was poet and Baptist minister, the Rev. Robert Ellis (Cynddelw), who greeted

Margaret with the following *englyn* (a strict metre four-line poem):

> *Pa beth? ai geneth o Ganaan – yw hon?*
>   *Mae'n hynod o ddyddan,*
>   *Ei dull wrth osod allan*
>   *Mor glir mewn Cymraeg lân.*

which translates:

> What's this? Is she the young girl from Canaan?
>   She's remarkably entertaining,
>   Her manner in setting out
>   So clearly in beautiful Welsh.

Margaret must have been delighted to hear that a well-regarded poet had composed a poem about her. For a Welsh person, it was the ultimate accolade.

Margaret continued to travel across mid and south Wales during the rest of 1871, but newspaper reports of the reaction to her lecture were becoming fewer and shorter in length; just a brief mention of the place and the date of her visit. She visited Bethlehem Chapel, Llangadog on 9 August and was in Pontypridd and Bridgend in late October. In early November, Sarah Jane Rees (Cranogwen) had started touring the country lecturing about her visit to the United States. And, it was *that* lecture now which attracted the attention of the newspapers.

But Margaret continued to travel, even in 1872, and west Wales would be her destination this time. In a short paragraph in *Y Tyst a'r Dydd* in late January, it was noted that the Welsh Lady from Canaan had spent the last three weeks delivering her lecture in Cardiganshire. Perhaps Margaret had asked the editor to include this paragraph in the newspaper as no-one else had recorded her lectures until then.[37]

But in early February, Margaret received a little more publicity. The correspondent, Ioan Glan Dewi, mentioned her visit to Nanternis, near New Quay. He was surprised at such a large turnout, because Margaret was scheduled to visit most of the chapels in the area.[38] Miss Jones had left quite an impression on him as well. He felt that far too many lecturers had the tendency to become flippant whilst entertaining their audience. But she did not – she spoke seriously whilst discussing her topic. This is an interesting remark; many other commentators had spoken of the light-heartedness of Margaret's lecture. Ioan Glan Dewi was also impressed with her simple style of dressing. He only wished that all the ladies of Nanternis would follow her example.

In early February, Margaret was back in Carmarthenshire, in Whitland on the first of the month and then Henllan Amgoed the following day. The correspondent, Gwilym Amgoed, was delighted to see that she looked so well, as she had travelled through south Wales in a great deal of bad weather. Gwilym Amgoed had seen her lecture three times, and thought that her delivery had improved each time.[39]

Margaret visited chapels in Cardigan, St Dogmaels and Capel Iwan before arriving at Newcastle Emlyn, on 20 February. There, she delivered her lecture in Ebenezer Chapel and a respectable number of people heard her according to the correspondent from the newspaper *Baner ac Amserau Cymru* [The Banner and Times of Wales]. It also noted that Margaret had already sent £700, an incredible amount in those days, to the Palestine Missionary Fund, and that she was hoping to send a further £300 in the near future.[40]

Then, Margaret travelled to Bryn Moriah in south Cardiganshire on 23 February. Perhaps it is there that she came across fellow-lecturer Cranogwen for the first time. This was Cranogwen's home area, and after the lecture Cranogwen recited four poems that she had composed about Canaan.[41]

Margaret continued travelling, securing lecturing engagements, and raising funds for the mission. But, in mid April 1872, she had a new experience whilst delivering her lecture, and it proved to be a very unpleasant event. Margaret's fame now meant that she could, on occasions, take on engagements outside the safe confines of chapel walls. And this is what happened in the smallest city in Great Britain, in St David's, Pembrokeshire. The Town Hall was hired for the lecture and a huge crowd came to listen to her. And that is how a problem arose. The hall was overflowing with people, and those at the very back could not hear Margaret speak. There was some commotion and this threw Margaret's composure. The audience had paid to hear her speak and many of them actually heard very little. Interestingly, the profits from that evening were shared between her Mission Fund and an appeal to help build a Congregational chapel in St David's.[42]

The experience was very disagreeable for Margaret. There are no newspaper reports of her delivering her lecture on Canaan after that. Perhaps the lecture had run its course. By then, Cranogwen, was travelling the country with a new lecture about Ann Griffiths. In early 1873, Thomas Levi had started lecturing on his experiences travelling through Egypt and Canaan. Perhaps there were no longer any areas of Wales which had not had the opportunity to hear her speak. After all, she had been on the road with the same lecture for nigh on two years. It was time for a break, for everybody concerned.

PART V

Africa and America

All through my life, I have longed for the sea. All comforts in the world were based on sailing the wide open oceans. But now I have changed my mind. You can divert yourself much better in the peace and quietness of the land.

(Margaret Jones, *Morocco, a'r hyn a welais yno*)

Margaret had been on British shores for ten years. She'd spent much of that time with her family, friends and the Bethlehem Chapel community in Rhosllannerchrugog. Margaret had achieved a great deal, had spread the word about Jesus Christ's love in Canaan and raised large amounts of money for the mission in the Middle East. But Margaret had itchy feet once more. Rhos's bleak, grey landscape had become rather tedious to the eye by now.

In 1879 Margaret started to make plans to take her lecture about Canaan to a new audience, in the United States. But one day that summer, she received two unexpected letters. One of them advised her to postpone her travel arrangements to America, as there were 'trouble in the works',[1] and the other letter was from her former employer, the Rev. E B Frankel. He was looking for someone to accompany his daughter, Elizabeth, who was about to move to Morocco. Margaret pondered over this opportunity to travel to Africa, to experience another potential adventure with someone who was already familiar to her. Despite some residual ill feeling towards the Frankel family, Margaret nevertheless accepted his offer.

In many ways this leap into the unknown would be far easier for her than the 1862 move when, as a mere twenty year-old she went to live in Paris, or as the twenty-two year-old, who boarded ship for Canaan in 1865. Margaret would have some command of the languages spoken in Morocco – Arabic and French. And Morocco wouldn't be that different from Canaan, surely? The landscape and climate would be quite similar and, in settling in Mogador, she would enjoy the experience of living near the Atlantic Ocean.

Mogador (which was renamed Essaouira in 1956 following Moroccan independence from France) was architecturally very impressive with picturesque stone ramparts, painted fishermen's boats and bright blue doors. Around three hours by car from Marrakesh, the town was founded by the Phoenicians in the seventh century BC. It was famed for a much-prized purple dye which was extracted from a local mollusc, the *murex*, a little offshore. At that time purple could not be produced and, as a result, exorbitant prices were charged for a dye of that colour. According to Aristotle, purple dye was worth ten to twenty times its weight in gold.

The Portuguese established a trade and military post in Mogador in the fifteenth century. But control of Mogador was lost to the Saadians and the town became less popular. In 1735, the French architect, Théodore Cornut, visited the town and injected fresh life into Mogador, adding European and Moroccan-style buildings to the town. It was renamed Essaouira, which means 'well designed'. The port grew, and gold, salt, ivory and ostrich feathers were exported to Europe. Today the town is a haven for tourists.

2

Margaret knew very little about Morocco. But she was aware that some missionary work was carried out there, mostly to convert Jews to Christianity. Jewish and Moroccan history had been intertwined since the first century AD when Jewish Berber communities settled in the country. In the centuries that followed, most Jewish communities were excluded from trading in Europe, so they came to live in Morocco and worked as farmers, metalworkers, dyers, glassblowers, bookbinders and cowboys. And when faced with even more persecution, inquisition and death in Europe from the fourteenth to the sixteenth centuries, many European Jews fled to Morocco. They did well under their tolerant Saadian masters. Jewish quarters, known as *mellahs*, were founded in many Moroccan towns, including Mogador.

The Frankel family had remained as missionaries in the Middle East. Elias Frankel left Jerusalem for London in January 1870 because of ill-health, but by September of the same year, he had returned to the Middle East as the Head of Mission in Damascus. He and his family lived there until 1873 when they returned to Marseilles in France for a year. Then, the opportunity arose for Frankel to work as the Head of Mission in Tunis in northern Africa. He commenced his work in May 1875, and he remained there until 1881, when he retired from missionary work.

When Margaret heard from her former master in the summer of 1879, he wasn't offering her employment as a family maid this time. He was, in fact, offering her two opportunities: a the chance to work as a teacher at a mission school in Morocco, and be a companion for his youngest daughter, Elizabeth, who had recently married the Rev. E B Shepherd in Tunis in June 1879. The young couple were about to move to work for the mission in Mogador, Morocco. Elizabeth was with child (a son was born to them in March 1880 in Mogador). But Elias Frankel couldn't give Margaret any further details, as he hadn't visited Mogador himself. And if Elias Frankel was aware of the desperate situation in Mogador, he certainly did not share the information with Margaret in that letter.

The LJS didn't have any representation in Morocco prior to 1875, when the Rev. J B Ginsburg arrived there from Algiers. And this is what he saw:

> ... much ignorance, superstition and fanaticism amongst the Jews... The Jews were also poor, and the temporal misery in the *mellah* indescribable, but they were very accessible, though their rabbis eventually offered a determined opposition to all missionary efforts.[2]

Despite the difficulties, no time was lost in establishing a school for boys, girls and adults. J B Ginsburg's wife started a Sunday school and a mothers' meeting, and services were held on Sunday and Friday evenings for converts, enquirers and their children, as well as a service for English residents. A year later, Bibles were being sold and over a hundred pounds had been raised for the mission.

The society was based at premises known as the Mizpeh and before too long many Jews were visiting its books dispensary. But, the chief rabbi was not happy that so many of his flock visited the Christians' building. Despite this, the society flourished in Mogador and the future looked very promising for the busy missionaries amongst the curious Jews.

But the missionary work suddenly came to an abrupt end on a Sunday in January 1877. That morning, a long procession of Jews, headed by several rabbis, made its way from the *mellah* through the *kasbah* (the Arab quarter), past the Mizpeh (the society's premises) to the Sultan's palace (the ruler of the town). And there, in a very confused meeting, the

Sultan was asked to expel all the missionaries of the LJS from Morocco. And in order to help the Sultan make his decision quickly, bullocks were slaughtered on the doors of those in authority. As the Sultan pondered over his decision, many Jewish leaders insisted that Jewish shopkeepers should not sell any produce to the inhabitants of the Mizpeh. They wanted to ensure that the missionaries, their families and friends starved within the walls of their compound. Any Jew caught breaking the rule and going near the Mizpeh, would be excommunicated. The schools suffered terribly, and missionary work in Mogador was paralyzed during the stand-off. However, the mission's workers and volunteers were in no personal danger at that time.

However, a change of heart came over the Jews in 1878 when more than 10,000 Jews and Muslims perished in Mogador in a terrible famine. Somehow J B Ginsburg and his fellow volunteers were able to relieve hundreds of starving Jews. This helped to ease tensions between the two groups. Ginsburg recounts:

> Every pound of rice, every loaf, or whatsoever else was offered to the famished Jew or Mohammedan, was a word spoken for Christ. For the first time in their lives, thousands became acquainted with the motives of Christian charity, and were impelled to enquire about Him who taught the Christian universal charity. Jews who formerly dreaded to approach your missionary, or who considered it sinful to listen to one who rejects rabbinical tradition, now came, not for the meat that perisheth, but to enquire into the Christian faith. Notable Jews have sent kind and grateful messages, and the chief rabbi himself sent a message of a similar kind.[3]

The famine was followed by a fever which swept through the town. Many of the mission's workers in the Mizpeh were laid low and the fever cost the life of one man, Solomon Darmon. Yet, even in these dire times, some Jews continued to plot against the missionaries, rather than concentrating on surviving the famine and fever. There were many examples of

Jewish opposition, despite the fact that the mission continued to be popular and was making good progress converting the minds of the Jews. The unfriendly attitude of the resident Consul didn't help matters either – he imprisoned one of the agents of the society. The fourth of February 1879 was a very difficult day: a Hebrew teacher in the school was excommunicated; he was robbed and subsequently turned out into the street. On the same day, one of the Jewish converts was seized, beaten and imprisoned. Those perpetrating these acts of violence moved from one offence to another. At the end of May, the local authorities decided to close the gates of the *mellah*, thus preventing the children from attending the mission school and reducing tensions.

However, most children were determined to attend school, and they took to climbing over the walls of the *mellah* in order to escape. Those who were seized were placed in irons, severely beaten and imprisoned. Their parents met the same fate for allowing their children to frequent the missionaries' school. One 66-year-old Jewess, who was a school servant, was seized, tortured and imprisoned. However, all this barbarous activity seemed only to strengthen the resolve of those Jews who wished to attend the Mizpeh. As a result, the tactics of their opponents became even more severe.

On 11 July 1879, a premeditated assault was made on the school children and adult Jews who were visiting the Mizpeh. Missionaries were now being attacked with stones. One member was seriously injured. But the perpetrators weren't punished for their crimes; instead, some of the workers of the Mizpeh were arrested. Five days later, some of the workers of the Mizpeh were banished from Morocco forever.

Margaret left Liverpool port on 21 September 1879, two months after some of the Mizpet workers had been exiled.

She travelled on her own on this occasion. The ship was bound for Gibraltar and that part of the journey would take six days. Margaret had a keen eye and, as she was travelling alone, she also had the time to watch everything that went on around her.

Margaret described her experiences aboard ship at the beginning of her book *Morocco, a'r hyn a welais yno* (1883). She soon gathered that there weren't any Welsh people aboard the ship. She came across half a dozen English people, whom she found to be rather unfriendly and unwilling to speak to her. And it is rather strange to hear such a religious lady making a joke at their expense in the book: two Englishmen meet an Irishman who notices that the coat of one of the Englishmen is on fire. Pat, the Irishman, asks the other Englishman why he didn't tell him that his coat was on fire and his response is because he hadn't been introduced to him! It seems that jokes about the English, Irish, Welsh and Scots were doing the rounds as early as the 1880s!

Margaret spent a week in Gibraltar, before crossing the Mediterranean Sea to Tangiers in Morocco, calling in the towns of Rabat and Casablanca before coming to her final destination of Mogador on 16 October.

3

In her introduction to the book *Morocco, a'r hyn a welais yno*, Margaret says that her reason for publishing it is because everyone should know something about every part of God's earth and its people. She tells her readers that this is the first Welsh book written about Morocco (and indeed, the only one which has ever been written in the Welsh language). This book differs from her letters from Canaan, as this is more of a guidebook than anything else; a book which contains many stories about what Margaret sees or hears during her time in Mogador, as well as extracts from her diary. There are chapters, in the form of short lectures, which discuss for example: the inhabitants of the country, their superstitions and rituals, Jewish and Moorish weddings, the famine of 1878, burial traditions, and so on.

When Margaret arrived at her home for the next three years, her first impression wasn't particularly favourable. Mogador was a town of 16,000 souls, with nearly half of them Jewish. Margaret complains that there is nothing beautiful about the town or the surrounding countryside. And, to a woman who is familiar with the green hills of Wales, she has to travel several miles to see any grass or trees at all. But she soon comes across some of the walled gardens in the eastern part of the town. There she sees vegetables growing and Margaret is struck by the *geranium* flowers which grow up to two yards in height. The gardens are home to many kinds of animals and birds: tortoises, monkeys, chameleons and parrots. The weather is the best thing about Mogador, in her opinion. It is never too hot or too cold at any time of the year. She wonders what the inhabitants have done to deserve living in a place with such a glorious climate.

Much of the book concentrates on the lives and the faith of people that she comes across on a daily basis. She works as a teacher in the mission school for the Jews, but it's not only Jewish people who are her regular companions; she knows enough to write quite authoritatively about the Moors, Negroes and Muslims also.

Margaret uses short stories to inform her readers and get her message across. She speaks very plainly, and often does not hold back at all, especially when she disagrees with the beliefs or behaviour of the locals. As a Christian in Mogador, she soon realises that she belongs to an unpopular minority in the country. It appears that Christians scare the children of the town. She mentions that little girls flee in tears because they have just seen a Christian. It seems that parents are responsible for spreading horror stories to their children, telling them about what Christians might do to them if they caught them. Margaret is quite sympathetic at times, as she knows that the Europeans can be quite overbearing when travelling around Morocco. She tells the story of British officials who came to visit Morocco with the blessing of the Sultan. Great banquets were organised wherever the officials visited. Their wishes were adhered to, even if it meant that the locals would have to go without food as a result of the visit. This was the list of food laid out for *one* evening's banquet: five large bowls of couscous, a pile of yeast cakes, a live sheep, fifty eggs and five pounds of butter. It's no surprise therefore that the locals distrusted the Europeans.

Margaret is particularly interested in the treatment of slaves. Most find their way to Mogador from an area around Timbuktu; food is left on the ground by the hijackers to entice them. They are then captured and led on foot to Morocco, a journey which can take more than six weeks. However, most don't survive this arduous journey, and if they do manage to reach Mogador, that is only the beginning of their worries. Young girls are raped by their new masters as soon as they are bought in the market in Mogador. Fifteen pounds is paid for a fit young male slave; six to eight pounds will be paid for a young woman in good condition and between a pound and fifteen pounds for an adult male, dependant on his age. Margaret's landlord tried to buy a 35-year-old woman and her child for three pounds. He had wanted to buy her to release her from slavery. But he was forbidden from doing so because he was a Christian. Only Muslims can purchase slaves. Margaret witnessed a young girl being bought by a 40-year-old man. She was then dragged through the streets to her new 'home'. She screamed and tried to get away. Margaret was appalled by the event. Without doubt, these stories would have been an eye-opener to her readers back in Wales.

Naturally, the Jews of Morocco captured most of

Margaret's attention. Jewish merchants created much of the wealth of the country. In Margaret's time, there were 7,000 Jews living in the Jewish quarter, the *mellah*, in Mogador. Most of them were destitute and came to Uxbar (where Margaret lived) to beg. Bread was the only food that Jews would accept from the hand of a Christian. Margaret would often leave leftovers from her meals for the starving Jews, but she soon discovered that they would rather die of famine than contaminate themselves with food cooked in the pots and pans used by Christians. However, starving Jews did not object to taking food from a Muslim and would eat it all, apart from the meat. Margaret, although angry with their attitude, also admires their personal sacrifice whilst showing loyalty to the commands of the rabbi.

Some of the richest Jews lived in Uxbar; but the vast majority lived in the *mellah*. The *mellah* was surrounded by high walls, as though leprosy was suffered by all, in Margaret's opinion. Margaret has the opportunity to visit the *mellah* and describes the unmentionable excrement which is piled two feet high against the walls and for a yard on each side of the narrow streets, with only a yard free in the middle so that one can walk. The drains are open, and the most wretched smell comes out of them and contaminates the air all around. This is where fevers start and plagues rise, and diseases of all kinds sweep thousands of *mellah* inhabitants to their deaths. As far as Margaret can tell, it's the young boys who get affected the most; their faces are sallow, thin and without spirit, and to complete the distressing image, their faces are pockmarked with smallpox.[4]

Margaret takes particular interest in the lives of Jewish women. Their rights are limited: for example, they are barred from leaving Morocco for fear that their husbands and Jewish children would follow them. Jewesses were treated badly. People often spat at them and Moorish children continually bothered them.

As she starts her work in the Mizpeh, Margaret comes across a great many Jews, some who want to 'return' – that is, become Christians – and those who have no desire to make such a change. She is very critical of the Jews, calling them superstitious and bigoted. The Jews are of the opinion that any fellow Jew who has 'returned' has committed a most heinous sin. She cites the example of a converted Jewess who lived in the same house as Margaret. The Jewess had a sister who worked as a prostitute. Their mother lived some distance outside Mogador, and she sent word asking her 'bad' daughter to return home. The 'bad' daughter was the one who had converted to Christianity; if she remained a Christian, she would no longer be regarded as her mother's daughter. Margaret gives another example, after seeing a group of Jews chasing a young Jewess along the streets of Mogador. The young Jewess had lost her headscarf and was running from the mob, trying to seek refuge at any door that would open to her. The mob was chasing her because she had been caught eating leavened bread during the Festival of the Unleavened Bread.

Margaret finds some of the Jewish rules perplexing. They turn a blind eye to theft. Margaret is the victim of a thieving whilst teaching the children in school one day. She decides not to mention the theft directly with the children in class. Instead, she tells them the story of the Ten Commandments. Having heard the story, the reaction of one of the children is to say that her mother has told her that stealing is not a sin, but that calling each other names *is* a sin. Margaret corrects her.

Margaret also describes Jewish traditions, such as placing five fingers of pitch on a wall to keep evil spirits away. Margaret notices an example of this on the wall above her own bed. The five fingers of pitch are to be found inside babies' cradles, boats, the heads of animals, and so on. If a birth is imminent in the family, a second coat of fingers of pitch is put on the whitewash. If a son is born, ten men of good standing will come to guard the baby and mother from sunset until sunrise for the next eight days, praying and singing all night long to keep the evil spirits away. No such supervision is necessary for baby girls. On the eighth day, the boy will be circumcised, and watched by someone constantly until his thirteenth birthday. Then a *bar mitzvah* is held. Margaret receives an invitation to one of these, and she listens to a young boy give a speech declaring that he is now a man. Margaret feels that an older person should be making such a vow.

Margaret has evidently done careful research for her travel guide. There are different chapters on several aspects of life in Morocco which contain many statistics. She knows of how the Moors came to live in Morocco, the fact that they are excellent craftsmen of goods made from gold and silver, and that they make wonderful carpets. She complains that the Islamic faith has lowered morals in the country, citing the example that Muslims are allowed to beat their wives if they have been unfaithful. Margaret shows that she is familiar with the Qur'an and quotes from it several times. She describes the dress of the Bedouin, and tells of their generous hospitality towards strangers. She is fascinated with the different foods available, the 'unusual' traditions of some of the tribes, for example, the Ishmaelite men who dry their wet or dirty hands in their beards, whilst their womenfolk dry their hands in their hair. Many customs infuriate her, such as women who must wait for their husbands to finish eating their meal, before they can eat the scraps left behind. And since Margaret has more contact with women, her abhorrence at the way they are treated is very clear. Indeed, Margaret is way ahead of her time in considering the lack of freedom amongst the women of the different tribes and faiths.

4

Margaret kept a diary of her visits to the Jews of the *mellah* and the following extracts were included in the book. They show the sorrowful state of the spirit of the Jews and their living conditions:

10 January 1880
Only twelve to fifteen children have attended the school in the past month, and only four of them are Jewish, a boy and three girls. Last week was distressing. The Jewish boy came to school for two days only. When I enquired as to why, I was told that he had not been fed, and that his father was bedridden due to lack of food. The three girls were in school all day yesterday; but they didn't go home to lunch, because it was too far, they said. In the afternoon, I gave them sewing work, but after sewing for an hour, one of the girls put her work down and started crying. 'What is the matter?' I asked. 'Why are you crying instead of carrying on with your work?' 'I cannot work anymore,' she said, 'I am too weak. I have not eaten anything today.' I asked her why they had stayed in school and not brought any food. 'We did not have any food to bring,' she said dolefully. I gave them all a piece of bread, and they ate it eagerly.

Last Friday, a boy called Leon stole money from my desk. His father was told, and he came to the school house with a leather strap, and gave his son the most wretched beating, which scared the other children as well. Everyone sat mute in their places as they were not sure, by the look on their faces, whether or not they would have to endure the same treatment. This was a good opportunity to tell them about the sin of stealing as it is, in their opinion, an inconsequential sin, if a sin at all.

11 January 1880

I went with Mr Ginsburg to the *mellah* today to see how some of the destitute were coping. We visited the Jewish boy who had been missing from school the previous week. His father had died of starvation and the son seemed to be hurrying towards the same wretched predicament. Arrangements were made for the future of the boy.

We saw the three girls dragging out their existence in poverty and squalor that I am unable to describe. The stench that arose from the damp detestation that had been dumped on the side of the narrow road was so strong that everyone, even those who are used to this sort of life, had placed some sort of scrap of material to their noses to stop them from inhaling such a wretched smell as this. This excrement was seeping into the doorway of the room where one of the most intelligent girls in the school lived. This was the only room that the family had and it housed father, mother, son and three daughters. If the door was shut, then the room would be in complete darkness, as there was no window at all, just a hole in the wall about a foot and a half long and half a foot wide. No fresh air came in through the window as it backed on to a dark road. The door was low and narrow and I had to bend low to get through it. I was so surprised that a sensible girl such as Mesauda had been brought up in such an unpleasant place. I looked on with admiration at the maiden, who tried so hard in such wretched circumstances.

Some time later, a Jew of good standing in the world came to the *mellah* and saw Mesauda. He was surprised by her intelligence and that she had learnt to read and write (something that was very rare among Jewesses). He asked for her hand in marriage and it was granted. But, the thing that surprises strangers like us, is that the man was already married and his wife lived in another town in Morocco. He sent a divorce letter to that poor woman, blaming her for her unreasonable behaviour: he could not bear to live with the 'unintelligent cow' any longer, having seen such a sensible and intelligent girl in Mesauda (who was only 13 years old at the time). But this was not the excuse that he wrote in the letter to the rabbi; he would not have succeeded in getting a divorce otherwise. The cost of the divorce letter was ten pence with a satisfactory excuse.

12 January 1880
I visited a family of Jewish girls in the *mellah* today. Through an interpreter, I relayed scriptural stories to them, as they were unable to read. They appeared to be very grateful and said that no-one had told them anything like this before, because Jewish girls rarely attended synagogue, only in the week that they marry and then once a year to kiss the Pentateuch. They did not have the presence of mind to think that the soul needed some spiritual nourishment, just as the body needs seasonal nourishment or food. At this time the father came in and I asked him, 'How come a man of your knowledge and abilities leaves his wife and children so uneducated? Do you not think that their souls are not as important or as valuable as your soul?' He was not sure about the *value* of their souls, but acknowledged without doubt, that they had souls. 'But,' the self-satisfied man said, 'it is not a custom amidst us to educate our women; their part in life is to marry and if we nourish their bodies for that, then the obligation of us fathers has been achieved. If men choose to educate their women after that, we have nothing to do with that.' I argued with him that that was not fair, as the girls would be mothers in due course, and if they knew nothing, then there would be no reason for the children to know anything, but I could not persuade him to see the benefits of changing his mind. I also spoke to him about the enactment of the prophecy, and that our Messiah *had* arrived. 'That was the Messiah of the Christians,' he said, 'having been born of a virgin. The Messiah of the Jews has not come. When He comes, everything will be restored,

even Canaan to the Israelites. The Jews here are the greatest enemies of the Christians and their religion, and we are always in continual danger when we accept visits from you; at the same time, *I* do think that the mission house is like a paradise garden in the middle of a wilderness.' I left having had the promise that he would read the prophecies about the coming of Christ with me on my next visit.

March 1880
I went on a visit to the *mellah* during Purim Festival. Seeing the woman grinding wheat, I asked in astonishment, 'Is it not a festival with you at the moment?' 'Yes.' 'Which festival?' 'Purim Festival.' 'Do you know its meaning?' 'Oh yes. In memory of Esther and Mordecai and Haman.' 'Good. Who was Esther?' 'Pharaoh's daughter.' 'Who was Mordecai?' 'Her brother.' 'Who was Haman?' 'Oh some bad man, the enemy of the Jews; we know that because our people draw ugly pictures of him and place them on the walls and shoot at him all day long. Did you not hear the sound of shooting today?' 'Yes.' 'Well, they were shooting Haman,' the women said, overjoyed that such a reprobate was being shot. 'What else do you know about Purim Festival?' 'No more. We have asked the rabbi many times during these festivals, but the only answer that we have ever been given is, "Read it for yourselves", but none of us can read, we have to stay here in a state of ignorance, as before.' Then I told them the whole story, and watched their expressions as they followed the fate of Esther, Mordecai and Haman, and the glorious ending for the Hebrews, which was enough payment for me having had to go through the excrement to meet them. They clapped their hands in exultation at the end saying, 'Now we can be joyful with all our hearts at the Festival of Purim, because we now know why we rejoice.'

On the 13th of the month, all the Jews fast. They go to their synagogues for most of the day, and the rabbi reads the book of Esther, and when they get to the name of Haman everyone claps their hands and bangs their feet, shouting in his memory.

4 April 1880
The school continues to grow in numbers; by now there are 30, with 14 of them being Jews. The three girls no longer come regularly, but do so when they are not needed in service. We hope that they will spread the 'Good news of great joy,' to the households where they are servants, and that the seeds sown will lead to an eternal life. The children learn English, French, Hebrew and Arabic; all these languages are essential in Mogador. The children also sing a Welsh hymn from the book of Mr Sankey,[5] that is, 'Yes, there is a country that is more beautiful than the sun'.

A Welshman, Commander Davies from Aberystwyth came to Mogador recently. He very kindly welcomed the older children and me on board his ship. All the ship's hands were Welsh speakers, and we sang many hymns to Sankey tunes. When the children heard us sing 'Yes, there is a country...' they were so enchanted that they begged me to teach the hymn to them, and they learnt it very quickly. There is something quite touching and dear about hearing the voices of African children singing in Welsh.

It is a joy to see their minds gradually developing. They ask a lot of questions in Bible class, which gives me a lot of satisfaction, because it shows that their minds are awake and that they are eager to learn. [...] Many drag themselves to school for the Bible class, even when they are all ill, and go home again after that class. [...]

The Jewesses of the *mellah* have very unusual ideas about their dress; they only seem to wear aprons made of patch-worked material. No girls will be seen wearing a bonnet, hat, shawl or jacket and very few wear slippers. It was uncommonly cold and rainy one day during my first winter in Mogador; the roads were deep in mud. It was wretched to see a poorly-looking 16-year-old girl going home from school to the *mellah*, half a mile away, through the mud in bare feet. So I gave her a pair of my own shoes, and ordered her to put them on her feet, which she did in my presence. But when she was nearing home, I heard that she had taken them off and carried them because she was too ashamed to wear them in front of acquaintances! [...]

I understood recently that there was a rich Jew in Uxbar who was very charitable and generous, especially to his fellow Jews in the *mellah*. When I got to know him, I asked if I could go with him to see the poor people that he felt sorry for.

'With pleasure,' he said, 'and I am glad that a woman takes so much interest in the Jews.' He called for me the following morning, and we visited nine families who lived (if you can call it living) in rooms with hardly any light to them. It was by way of light from matches that we could tell who lived in each room. One room was a yard and a half wide by three yards long. I went in, leaving Mr — outside, when suddenly my shoulder was grabbed by a woman who said excitedly, 'Don't put your foot on her!' 'On who?' I asked. 'On the sick woman and her two children lying on the floor,' she said. I lit a match, and there, to my astonishment, I saw a poor woman lying on a sack on the floor, with nothing covering her but an old scrap of a shirt, and her day-old twins by her side. The scene was shocking; it was difficult not to cry. Oh, Israel, how have you come to this; how have your beautiful daughters come to this! The *Royal Children*, the children chosen by the King of heaven and earth as His *pets*. How long will you, the God of Israel, hide your face from them? I lit match after match, as there was nothing else to light the room. I spoke, but the mother was too ill to take any notice of anyone around her. I gave the children a few things I had with me. 'Where is the father of these poor things?' I asked the lady who had touched me on the shoulder. 'He has run from the country and has married another woman.' Mr — and I went to fetch a doctor, food and organise a nursing-home for the abandoned. 'Oh Mr — ,' I said, 'what a wretched sight.' 'That is but small in comparison to much that I have seen, especially since the famine.'[6]

Margaret felt hopeless about the situation of the Jews, especially the way in which Jewish mothers and daughters were treated. She wasn't at all concerned for her own safety when she found herself in difficult situations – she was eager to see for herself the horrors that others had mentioned to her. It is hard to tell if Margaret's work did any lasting good amongst the Jewesses of Mogador. One wonders how they reacted to her, this determined foreign woman with such a sharp tongue. As an individual it would have been very challenging to change the hearts and minds of Jewish men with regard to the future of their wives and daughters. But, as she departed Morocco in the autumn of 1882, Margaret was sincerely hoping that she had left some sort of legacy and made the lives of some of the residents of Mogador a little more tolerable.

5

Margaret returned to Wales in October 1882. She was very tired, both mentally and physically, and much in need of a rest. She was not in the best of health either after several years living on the African continent.[7] Just before Christmas 1882, Margaret returned to her father's house in Rhosllannerchrugog once more, and set about putting her thoughts and experiences of Morocco down on paper, so that they could be published in due course.

Unlike *Llythyrau Cymraes o Wlad Canaan*, these memoirs would not be printed in the columns of a Welsh newspaper. Margaret hoped that the fact that she was already well known in Welsh religious circles would encourage people to buy a new book about her experiences. The book would be publicised, not as the writings of Margaret Jones, but as the musings of the 'Welsh Lady from Canaan' about Morocco.

Hughes & Son from Wrexham printed the book but any other work, such as promoting the book, fell on Margaret's shoulders. An advertisement in the Welsh Congregationalist weekly newspaper, *Y Tyst a'r Dydd* on 9 March 1883, announced:

> Now available, priced one shilling
> The book of the 'Welsh Lady from Canaan' on Morocco.
> Send all orders to the father of the Welsh Lady,
> Mr Owen Jones, Hall Street, Rhosllan, Ruabon.[8]

Amongst other advertisements, such as one for 'Stephens' Stomach and Liver pills', an advert publicising Margaret's book appeared three times in the newspaper, and twice in *Baner ac Amserau Cymru* in the same month. But, the book was not listed in the large advertisement of new books on sale from Hughes & Son in the same newspaper. In truth, Margaret was a self-published author and her father, who now called himself a bookseller, was confident enough to sell his daughter's publication on his own.

It is quite clear that Margaret's adventures, and others like her, spurred many to write about their experiences. Just by browsing through denominational newspapers of the day, for example *Y Tyst a'r Dydd* in 1883, one comes across many correspondents doing very much the same thing as Margaret, from all parts of the globe. For instance, in a March edition there is a 'Letter from a Welsh Lady in China'; in June a 'Lesson from America' by H E Thomas, Pittsburgh; T Penry Evans of Pontarddulais writes of the 'Mission in Tanganyika'; in August a piece was written about the 'Missionaries of Madagascar' and finally, the Rev. Morris Thomas writes a letter from India about his work spreading the 'Word' there. It appears that all points of the compass, in the northern and southern hemispheres, were represented in Welsh newspaper reports.

After a flurry of advertising in March, there is no further mention of Margaret's book in later editions of the newspaper that year. And, despite there being the occasional book review column in *Y Tyst a'r Dydd*, it is left to another publication to review the book. *Morocco, a'r hyn a welais yno* was reviewed in June 1883 in the monthly magazine *Y Cronicl* [The Chronicle] which was published in Bala.[9] The magazine was edited by the Rev. J Roberts, Conwy, and it seems that he may have reviewed the book too, as no name appears at the end of the piece.

The reviewer isn't particularly kind. He spends most of the review giving his own opinion of the work of missionaries who work all over the world. He has little which is good to say about them. And of Margaret herself, he writes that the Welsh lady has eyes in her head, but that she seems to see far too much with them! A little more complimentarily, he adds that she has a real talent for visualizing images, but that her grammar and syntax in her descriptions are poor. He gives his readers a little of Margaret's background, adding that she doesn't seem to have had much success with her missionary work, if her words in this book are to be believed. The reviewer ends by stating that the lasting impression of the Welsh lady's book is of the grandeur of false religion, the suffering of the world, and the failings of missionary work. In truth, more than half of the review has very little to do with Margaret's book at all.

But, at least Margaret's book had been reviewed this time, and she'd received a little more publicity as well. And there would be more attention as she organised a few dates to deliver a lecture about her time in Morocco. But surprisingly, from what has been gleaned from the press at the time, there weren't as many dates for lecturing in the diary this time. She delivered her first lecture on Morocco before the book was published in March 1883. In January of that year, at a chapel in Pen-y-bont-fawr, Montgomeryshire, the 'Welsh Lady' (as she was increasingly referred to), kept the congregation happy for over two hours speaking about 'Hynodion gwlad Morocco a'i thrigolion' (The peculiarities of Morocco and her inhabitants). In a similar fashion to her lectures on Canaan, Margaret had brought with her three examples of outfits worn by the ladies of Morocco. The newspaper *Y Tyst a'r Dydd* reported that the 'models' had done their work very well and that Margaret seemed to be in excellent spirits whilst delivering her lecture.[10]

On 15 March, in the week when the book was finally available to be purchased, Margaret repeated the lecture at the Congregational chapel in Llanbryn-mair. The chairman of the evening, Mr J Jones, had travelled twenty miles from Aberdyfi for the sole purpose of listening to the Welsh Lady. And, according to the *Baner* correspondent, having sung a hymn, Margaret rose to her feet and told her audience about her journey via Gibraltar and Tangiers to Mogador; the local customs of marriage, dressing, worshipping and eating, and she showed three costumes which were a wedding gown, an outfit that would be worn during the day and an outfit for very hot weather. The commentator noted that the Welsh Lady had certainly seen strange things and had done great things. A profit of £12 was made, which was *quite* good![11]

Rather surprisingly, this was the only newspaper source discovered about Margaret's new lecture. There were still plenty of opportunities to travel the country and speak to chapel audiences. The religious Welsh had not lost their appetite for attending lectures. In 1883, the Rev. David Oliver of Treffynnon was enjoying very many column inches in the newspapers with his lecture about the links between the British Government and the opium trade in China. Indeed, as was the Rev. O Jones of Pwllheli, who was travelling across the country speaking about his journey to Palestine.

But, as in the summer of 1879, Margaret was once again keen to go to America. She'd been persuaded to postpone on that occasion, and anyway, she'd had an offer to go to Morocco at the same time. But now, with nothing pending and no other opportunities arising, the idea of travelling to America was becoming more appealing by the day.

6

It was not particularly difficult or expensive to secure a passage to America in the 1880s. Advertisements appeared regularly in the Welsh press offering new lives and opportunities in many parts of North America. For example, the following advertisement was to be seen in *Y Tyst a'r Dydd* in 1883, offering a voyage on one of the Dominion Line's ships out of Liverpool every Thursday:

> Reduced rates from Liverpool on Thursdays. This line books
> passengers through to all parts of America. At Special Low Rates.
> Saloon from £10.10s. Intermediate £8. Steerage £4.4s. Assisted
> Passages are granted to Manitoba, the North West Territory and
> to all parts of Canada. Assisted Ocean Rates for Agricultural
> Labourers, their families and Female Domestic Servants, £3 per
> adult; Mechanics, Navvies, General Labourers and their families
> £4. Children under 12 years £2. Infants under one year 10s.[12]

Advertisements such as these were aimed at individuals and families looking for a new life, with one-way tickets being sold mostly. But, unlike the majority, Margaret wanted a return ticket because she did not have the comfort of knowing that someone familiar would be waiting for her at the end of her journey this time. However Margaret, like most other newspaper readers in Wales, was well aware of news and events in America. Newspapers such as *Y Tyst a'r Dydd* included regular columns mentioning the contents of American newspapers. And personal correspondence did not take long to travel from one shore to another either.

In the spring of 1883, with her latest book beginning to sell well, Margaret corresponded with a few people from the Congregationalist movement who would be able to help her once she arrived in New York. In that city, she secured some lodgings and a few engagements to deliver her lecture. Like Sarah Jane Rees (Cranogwen) before her, she boarded a ship bound for New York, and this on 12 May 1883.

Margaret sailed with the Cunard Line on the steam ship *S/S Bothnia (1)*.[13] With the ship sailing at a speed of twelve and a half knots, Margaret arrived in New York City harbour eight days later on 20 May.[14] There, she was greeted by a few Welsh Americans and Margaret spent the next few weeks in the city delivering her lecture four times to Welsh audiences. In June she travelled to Utica in New York State, another popular destination for the migrating Welsh.[15] Later, in October, according to a note in the newspaper *Y Genedl Gymreig* [The Welsh Nation], Margaret praised the welcome that she had received in the United States from Welsh Americans, reasoning that it was mainly due to the fact that she was a woman![16] But after that, Margaret's trail in America disappears completely. She had arrived in America at a time when ease of travel around the country was improving greatly; for example, the Brooklyn Bridge in New York was opened four days after her arrival.[17] Therefore, it was now much easier to get around the country than it had been for Cranogwen over ten years earlier.

According to Margaret's obituary, published in the *Queensland Times* at the time of her death in October 1902, she spent two years in America. It is strange, if she did indeed spend that length of time there, that she did not record on paper any of her experiences in the country. The Welsh American newspapers and magazines were searched thoroughly, yet there is no account of her lecturing anywhere (other than the notes in the Welsh press saying that she had arrived safely in New York and travelled on to

Utica). Two years later, in June 1885, there is a paragraph in *Y Tyst a'r Dydd* which mentions that the office of *Y Tyst* has received many letters in the past year enquiring as to the whereabouts of the Welsh Lady. The newspaper assures the admirers of the Welsh Lady that they should send any letters to her home as follows: The Welsh Lady from Canaan, Rhos, Ruabon. The newspaper does not mention the recent movements of Margaret, nor when she returned from her visit to America.[18] And indeed, possibly in response to those enquiries in *Y Tyst*, Margaret delivers her lecture about Morocco one more time on 26 June 1885 in Cerrigydrudion.[19]

For a lady who'd been a frequent letter writer and kept a detailed diary whilst travelling in the past, this lack of information about her time in America is very bewildering. Perhaps Margaret was of the opinion that the public weren't that interested in her anymore. Perhaps she didn't have the energy to record every minute detail of her life and go through the tiring process of publishing and lecturing. Perhaps the opinions of the critics or some of her detractors back home in Wales had persuaded her to keep quiet about her experiences. Perhaps her own personal star wasn't quite as bright as before.

PART VI

Australia

The site of the house commands a most picturesque view of the surrounding country, as far as the watershed which separates the waters of the Oxley and Opossum Creeks and thence to Mount Flinders. The natural scenery of the place is magnificent, and that which crowns the whole is a fine lagoon in front of the building, from the edge of which the land rises gently to the summit of the mountain.

(*Queensland Times*, April 1876)

The following announcement appeared five times in *Y Genedl Gymreig* in August and September 1888:

> From 'The Welsh Lady from Canaan' to the Welsh public. As I am about to leave Wales in order to reside in Australia, I wish to make it known that Messers. Hughes & Son of Wrexham have a number of copies of my books *Morocco, a'r hyn a welais yno* [Morocco, and what I saw there] (Price 1s.) and *Llythyrau Cymraes o Wlad Canaan* [The Letters of a Welsh Lady from Canaan] (Price 6d.), or both bound together in an attractive cloth for 2s. 6d.
>
> P.S. As there are only a few copies left, you are encouraged to send your orders in as soon as possible.

That autumn, Margaret made preparations for the longest journey, and as it turned out, the last international journey of her life. She was now approaching 47 years and, having had a short respite, her appetite for seeking out new horizons in life had not waned. But Margaret was not the first in the family to travel to this distant land. Her half-sister, Mary Anne, was already a resident of Ipswich, near Brisbane in the state of Queensland. The plan was that Margaret would join her and live with her.

Although Margaret had family in Australia, what were the other reasons for leaving Wales for ever and emigrating to Australia in 1888? Several years had passed since she'd returned from the United States. She was very fond of the Middle East and her dearest wish at one time had been to return there. But she did not. After spending time in America, she returned to Wales to look after her family and deliver a few lectures. Her father was an old man and a widower three times over by now. He died at his home in Hall Street, Rhosllannerchrugog on 31 March 1887, at 71 years of age, as a result of severe bronchitis, a condition associated with working underground for many years.

Within six months of his death, his youngest child, Mary Anne, who was eighteen years old at the time, decided that there was no future for her in Rhos, nor in Wales. Mary Anne sailed out of London on 5 November 1887 on the *Duke of Sutherland* bound for Brisbane. Fourteen months later, in January 1889, Margaret would do the same.

Margaret and Mary Anne and indeed a brother, Owen, were following a migration pattern which had commenced in Wales more than fifty years earlier. The reasons for migration were largely the same throughout the nineteenth century. But the end of the journey for the Welsh covered all points of the compass.

In 1840s rural Wales, for example, families young and old tried to escape from poverty and low expectations in farming by seeking a new life, not only in the coal mining areas of south and north-east Wales, but also in London, establishing milk round businesses. But, to those raised on strict Nonconformist hearths, the lax lifestyles and low morals of such places were very unattractive. Many brave Welsh people decided to cross the Atlantic and start afresh there, establishing Welsh enclaves in states such as Ohio and Pennsylvania. Between 1840 and 1865, for example, three-quarters of the population of the community of Mynydd Bach in Cardiganshire sailed out of Liverpool for the eastern seaboard of the United States.

Argentina also appealed a great deal. It has already been mentioned that there was talk of establishing a Welsh colony in Canaan in the 1850s. As the United States was americanising the Welsh so quickly, it was decided to find another location for a Welsh colony. On 25 May 1865, with the encouragement of the religious leader Michael D Jones, around 160 Welsh souls sailed on the *Mimosa* and landed in New Bay, Patagonia on 28 July. It had been a torrid journey – and life was particularly difficult for the new settlers, especially in the early years. But the Welsh weren't people who gave up easily, and a Welsh colony was successfully established on the banks of the river Chubut. Many were encouraged to follow in their footsteps and Welsh is still spoken there to this day.

Another southern hemisphere country attracted the Welsh in the nineteenth century, but not in the hope of improving their way of life, it seems. Around 1,900 Welshmen and 300 Welshwomen were sent to Australia between the years 1788 and 1868. Australia was a penal colony at the time and that was the reason for sending over 2,000 Welsh people there. Some of them had participated in the Rebecca Riots, when poor farmers and smallholders were incarcerated for destroying the tollgates of new roads constructed all around Wales.

Later, many thousands of Welsh people migrated to Australia of their own free will. Work, especially mining copper and gold in the states of Victoria and New South Wales, attracted thousands of migrants in the 1840s and 1850s. But by the 1870s, it was work in the coal mines which brought ship-loads of Welsh people willing to undertake the long journey to Australia. And one coal mining area was particularly popular with the Welsh, the area which surrounded the town of Ipswich in Queensland.

It was a Welshman, Lewis Thomas (1832–1913), who was born in Tal-y-bont, Cardiganshire, who first saw the potential to develop a lucrative coalfield in the Ipswich area. As a nine year-old in Wales, he'd been sent to work in a woollen factory; by the age of fifteen he was working the lead mines of Esgair and later he worked in the coal and iron mines of south Wales. He emigrated to Australia in 1859, leaving his wife Ann behind in Wales until 1877.

He sailed for Victoria and initially panned for gold. But he soon realised that he wasn't going to make his fortune in this way, therefore he moved northwards to Queensland in April 1861. He worked on the railways for a while, before turning his attention to the burgeoning coal mining industry. Lewis Thomas discovered much of the West Moreton coalfield. He opened the famous Aberdare Colliery at Bundamba which would, at its height, produce between 50,000 and 60,000 tonnes of coal a year. He opened another mine at Dinmore in 1870 and, with the extension of railways in Queensland, a huge demand for coal was created. This boosted Lewis Thomas's fortunes further and earned him the title of 'Coal King' of Ipswich.

News of Lewis Thomas's success wasn't slow in reaching Wales. This stimulated much more Welsh emigration to Queensland. In 1883 a large group of former slate miners from Blaenau Ffestinog went there. By 1891, Lewis Thomas had built Brynhyfryd, a mansion which overlooked the coalfields. A short distance away, the new Welsh village of Blackstone was erected. Lewis Thomas did his best to strengthen the Welsh community in Blackstone and the village became the centre of Welsh cultural life in Queensland. Thomas worked in coal mining until his retirement. He was then elected a Member of Parliament for Bundamba from 1893 to 1899.[1]

And one of the reasons why Blackstone became a

centre for the exiled Welsh was the establishment of a
Welsh chapel. Shortly after the arrival of the slate miners
from Blaenau Ffestiniog, they held a Protestant service
under a mulberry tree on the banks of Bundamba Creek.
They agreed that Welsh nationality would take priority
over minor denominational differences, and so formed
the United Welsh Church. The first service was held in a
church hall in the nearby suburb of Newtown on 19 July
1883. Lewis Thomas then allowed the use of a cottage in
Blackstone for services. As the number of those attending
services grew, Lewis Thomas donated land for the erection
of a chapel. The chapel was officially opened on 1 October
1886.

Blackstone United Welsh Church would become the
cornerstone of Welsh life in Queensland. It held singing
festivals, eisteddfodau and clubs. The first singing festival
was held at the chapel in 1902 and it is still a biennial
event. The first eisteddfod was held on New Year's Day
1887, a few months after the building had been opened.
A local choir was formed for the eisteddfod and that also
continues to this day; it is known as Blackstone-Ipswich
Cambrian Choir.

2

Margaret bade farewell to the country of her birth for the
last time in January 1889. She boarded the ship *Jumna 1886*
in London on 11 January. The ship's records say that her age
was 44 years, but, in fact, she was about to turn 47 years. In
the nineteenth century the Queensland government tried to
attract young women of childbearing age to the colony in
order to increase the population, and this is why Margaret's
half-sister, Mary Anne, was welcomed to Australia as a 'free
passenger',[2] at the age of 18 in 1888. But Margaret was older
and an 'assisted passenger'.[3]

The journey on the *Jumna 1886* was long and

uncomfortable. After nearly two months at sea, Margaret disembarked in Brisbane on 4 March 1889. As Margaret was an 'assisted passenger', it is worth asking who contributed to pay for Margaret's sea voyage. According to the rules, a resident of Australia had to pay a sum of money to the government to secure a passage warrant for an immigrant to enter Australia. It is not known exactly how much this sum was. It is unlikely that her half-sister Mary Anne's financial circumstances would allow her to help Margaret, although she had arrived in Queensland a year earlier. It appears that Mary Anne spent some time in Brisbane, before moving to Ipswich and securing work in a shop called Cribb & Foote, commencing work on 7 November 1888.

It is more likely that Margaret had some sort of promise of work in Australia before she left Wales, and perhaps it was her new employers who paid the monies towards the passage warrant. A day after Margaret arrived in Brisbane, a special meeting of the Central Congregational Church, Ipswich was held, where the minister, the Rev. Joseph Walker, recommended Margaret as a suitable 'Bible woman' for the church. It seems that the minister had met Margaret at the port a day earlier, and had decided that the reports he had heard of her were accurate and that it would be worthwhile giving her a trial period of work.

If this is true, this venture had been a huge gamble for the church. They would have probably paid a sum of money towards Margaret's voyage already. There was no guarantee that Margaret would have sailed, and they weren't sure either if Margaret was suitable for the post. The deacon's minutes of the Central Congregational Church mention that a Mr Baines had said that there was a need for a 'Bible woman' and a Scripture reader in the church, on 30 January 1889, when Margaret was, incidentally, already half way through her voyage to Australia. A further note in the minutes from 5 February says that, while it is the duty of all Christians to visit those who are sick at home, the deacons think it best that women should visit those who were unable to attend church due to illness, old age or any other reason. And this, in essence, would be Margaret's work.

In the special meeting held on 5 March, it was agreed that Margaret should be offered an agreement of work for six months, at a salary of 30 shillings a week. It was also noted that this was not to be a permanent agreement, because the church needed to employ an assistant minister or evangelist to work in an area called Rosewood. The church would not be able to support a minister, an assistant and a Bible woman. If Margaret had been persuaded to come to Australia on the basis of the work offered by the Central Congregational Church, then she had travelled very far with very little on offer to her. It took until 1 April to agree terms. Margaret started her work as the Bible woman two days later.

3

Central Congregational Church, Ipswich was established on 2 June 1854 in a wooden-built chapel; this was the first Congregational church in Queensland. The congregation grew in the 1860s and a new chapel was built at a cost of £2,000. Much like Bethlehem Chapel in Rhos, this chapel also had a valuable pipe organ, bought at a cost of £300 in 1881. The Congregational Church was forward-looking and innovative and this is shown by Margaret's appointment. The church also had branches in other areas and the first purpose-built Sunday school building in the southern hemisphere.[4]

Margaret commenced her duties as a Bible woman on the same day as a letter of recommendation arrived from a chapel in Wales (one presumes that this was Bethlehem Congregational Chapel in Rhosllannerchrugog), endorsing Margaret for the appointment. All the deacons were now happy to allow Margaret to commence her work. Three weeks later, Margaret was requested to show her employers a diary of how she kept her time and whom she visited. Her diary survives to this day and is to be found at the John Oxley Library in Queensland. It is a small leather covered notebook of plain paper, entitled 'Miss Jones' Lady Visitors Diary of Work'. Margaret had numbered the pages up to 155.

From reading the diary, it is obvious that her work was to visit local households and encourage adults to attend the Central Congregational Church and the children to come to Sunday school. Each entry gives the date of the visit and some names and addresses of those whom she met. She discusses the families' circumstances: the father who is always drunk, or ill, or without work, or in trouble with the law. Then, she records the names of those who have said that they would consider attending the church or sending their children to the Sunday school. The diary gives an insight into the lives of those living in Ipswich in 1889 and the lengths that the church, especially the Congregational Church, went to try to engage them to attend worship.

Margaret's diary commences on Wednesday, 3 April, barely a month since her arrival in Australia. Margaret attempts to get her bearings quickly and she is told to call on a Miss Berry and a Miss Perkins, who are to introduce her to people. Unfortunately they are too busy to help her and so Margaret ventures out on her own. She comes across a German housewife who tells Margaret that she and her husband are members with the Baptist Church. The lady also adds, perhaps rather ruefully, that there will be *plenty* of work for Margaret in the neighbourhood!

During the next six months, Margaret kept a keen eye on the members of the varying denominations that she came across. At the end of most diary entries was a tally of how many Congregationalists, Anglicans, Wesleyans, Baptists, Salvation Army, Primitive Methodists or Roman

Catholics she had met. Naturally, she met a great number of Congregationalists, but she also came across very many Roman Catholics. On only her second day in the job, she did not hold back on her general opinion of them:

> ... then I came to a Roman Catholic and oh! didn't the woman snub me! She said in a very scowling manner, walking away as she did so, that she went to her own chapel and no one need look after her. The idea! How absurd! I came upon several Catholics after this but they were all civil.[5]

Margaret seems to have some strong preconceived ideas about members of the Church of Rome. In September 1889 she writes:

> One house was so large and grand that I could not have guessed it to be inhabited by Roman Catholics. The lady was very kind but said, 'Our church is but one, we have not many sections, we are true to that church, but if anyone leaves it, we grieve not, as he would have been no good to us, nor will he be good to any other church.' I did not contradict her.
>
> Another Roman Catholic was a drunken sort of a woman. 'Go', she said staggering. 'You don't believe that our Blessed Virgin Mary was more than a woman. You think you can get to heaven without her. Go.' And I went.[6]

It is obvious that there was a great deal of mistrust between various denominations in Ipswich in 1899. Margaret mentions the thoughts of others that she met, as on 18 June:

> The other Protestants were Church members, one of them an English Church woman and owning house property, she complained sadly of the persecution she has suffered from the Roman Catholics, she being the only Protestant in the street.[7]

But some Protestants and Catholics evidently got on much better. Mixed marriages were very common in Ipswich, but the repercussions were difficult to manage as Margaret notes on 2 July:

This woman was brought up a Catholic, but married a Protestant
in a Protestant Church. On that account, when the first child
was born, the mother took it to the priest for baptism, but his
Reverence refused to officiate and spurned both mother and child.
Since then (11 years ago), the father and children have attended
the English Church, where all the children have been christened.
On these occasions only does the mother ever enter a place of
worship.[8]

Margaret's brief from her employers at the
Congregational Church was to call at houses in various
parts of Ipswich without an invitation. This was unpleasant
work, on the whole, as Margaret had no idea what would
confront her as she knocked on the doors of unfamiliar
houses. But Margaret had been hardened by the years
spent in Jerusalem and Mogador with people who did not
share her ideals, and she had also survived the odd heckler
at public speaking engagements. After all, in Australia she
had a message and she was determined to deliver it. When
she met someone for the first time, she would get to her
point immediately, which undoubtedly must have been
very off-putting. In her diary, she mentions about coming
across a family she'd been advised to 'take in hand':

A family had been pointed out to me, a harsh drunken family
which ought to be taken in hand. On arriving, I found that
the parents were not at home, but they had left a very true
representative in the person of a son about 15 years old.
  'Do you attend the Little Ipswich Church on Monday
evenings,' I asked?
  'No, why? I have nothing to say to such things.'
  'Do you *never* go to church?'
  'No.'
  'Do you know that you have a soul inside you, that will live
forever either happy, or intensely miserable?'
  Silence.
  'Do you think yourself man enough to do without God?'
  'I cannot stand here,' he said. 'I must go to my work.'
  And off he went to the back of the house, muttering all the

way. His little sister appeared. I knew her at once as a constant attendant at the children's evening meetings on Mondays. The future of the boy is horrible to think of.[9]

From her diary, it seems that children were often pushed forward to deal with Margaret when she was on her visiting rounds. As parents cowered in the back rooms of houses, Margaret often found herself dealing with children on the doorstep. She found herself in the role of social worker to many families, having to deal with drunken adults and out of control children as well:

> One of the women I had visited before wished me to take
> her little daughter for a week to try and manage her, that she
> would gladly pay me; certainly the child did behave shockingly
> and defied her mother in my presence. Then she put the child
> (four year old) in a room by herself and shut her in, where she
> kicked and screamed fearfully. I asked permission to go to her
> which was readily granted. I shut the door on our two selves. I
> managed to tame her, but she would not kneel down and did not.
> I found out it was all the fault of training. Pity! Have promised to
> call soon again.[10]

It seems that Margaret would come across situations that she described as being hopelessly desperate on a daily basis. Margaret certainly meant well in all her endeavours but it didn't always seem that her efforts were much appreciated. She comes across this family less than a month into her role:

> The first of the other ten called upon was the notoriously
> bad woman. My approach was noticed but not before I saw
> how matters stood. The woman was lying down in a state of
> intoxication (as I understood by her utterances afterwards)
> and a young woman stood by with a baby on her arm. As soon
> as my approach was detected, there was a rush and the door
> and window of the room banged to. In answer to my knock,
> a boy, about 14 or 15 came toward the door. 'You will let me
> see your mother today won't you,' I said, 'because I know
> that she is in.' The boy put a 'We are caught!' sort of grin on,

then entered the mother's room as if to ask a question. In a moment he returned and said, 'Mother is not well today and can't see you.' Tell your mother I come to see sick people. He returned again and I thought he never would come out this time. I stood leaning on the door post a quarter of an hour waiting an answer, as I was determined if possible to see her. But no, I was not to have my wish. I could hear every word she said, and understood they were drunken utterances. What a dreadful language! What a pity any *woman* could allow anything so degrading to pass her lips, especially before children – *her own children*! I feel as if the word 'mother' were in mourning. I think we ought to make this case a subject for prayer. The boy appeared at last saying I could not see his mother. Leaving a message inviting her to see me, that I wished to make a friend of her, I departed sad at heart. Then I called with a Christian old lady, whom I was told had an influence over this wretched woman. By what this lady said, the case is hopeless. Still there is nothing beyond the power of God and we can try.[11]

It's not surprising that people went into hiding as they saw Margaret coming towards their front door. In some households her arrival may have been thought of as the end of the world being nigh. She was often bluntly asked who she was and what she wanted. Often, her replies gave plenty for the unsuspecting to start worrying:

I called at one house where a youngish woman opened the door. As I spoke, her black, piercing eyes glistened. So then she called,
    'Father! Father! Come here quick. There is a lady here talking so nice.'
    'I don't want ladies,' answered the invisible father.
    'But you must come to her.'
    I thought his daughter's conduct rather strange. However, the old man came after a while, feeling his way along the passage though his eyes were wide open. I rose and going to him laid my hand on his shoulder.
    'Let me help you,' I said.
    'Who are you?' he asked.
    'I am a messenger from God,' I answered, 'to ask if your soul

is washed in the blood of the Lamb. Are your feet on the Rock of Ages?'

The old man burst out crying, and pitifully wailed, 'I am blind. I cannot see you. No, my soul is not washed. I am not on the Rock, but I want to be.'

'Come,' I said, 'I will try to help you to the right way.'

'Not today,' he answered. 'I cannot stand it today. I am too much overcome. Call again.'

I found after leaving this house that the daughter who opened the door is deranged in her mind.[12]

The tidings of the 'Messenger from God' would at times be completely inappropriate. Margaret was occasionally accused of being heartless and what she said was open to misrepresentation. She relates in her diary:

> One I visited was a very flighty little woman, a plague to her neighbours. She accused me of saying to her after the death of her child about a month ago that that was a warning to her to give her heart to Christ and if she does not obey now, God will *surely* take another. I am very *certain* that I never uttered nor yet thought the last sentence, which she says Mrs Bennett considered very wrong and inconsiderate of me. This is the first accusation of this kind. I suppose misinterpretations will happen, however careful one may be.[13]

These misunderstandings would often make Margaret feel very depressed. Her spirits were low within a fortnight of starting her new position when she writes, 'I left home today feeling depressed. These people withdrawing from their promises made me unhappy, and the callous acquiescence of many to whatever I may say is worse than all.'[14] But her work would also give her great satisfaction. She also writes in her second week of having a 'busy, pleasant day, profitable to my own soul. In trying to water others, I have myself been watered'[15] and 'we had a long conversation, that did me much good and they seemed well pleased'.[16]

Margaret would often come across people from her native Wales. She met Mrs Lewis Thomas, the wife of the coal baron, soon after arriving in Australia. Mrs Thomas worshipped at the two Welsh chapels established by her husband in Blackstone, and so, she could not be persuaded to join the congregation in Ipswich. But most of the other Welsh people that she met were not as privileged nor as wealthy as the Thomases. And hearing the Welsh language spoken had a mesmerizing effect on some of the hardened Welsh souls that Margaret tried to persuade to turn to God:

> I visited one woman who proved to be Welsh. Her children attend our Sunday school, but the mother never goes anywhere (father dead). She received me hard, if not defiant at first, but when I spoke her own language, she gave me a quick look of surprise and pleasure and we became friends at once. I hope under God's blessing to be of some comfort and edification to the poor widow. I failed to get her to promise to come to church next Sunday. The habit of staying at home is so strong on her.[17]

The best way of getting women and children to attend the church was to hold mothers' meetings, and Margaret was central in establishing these. Going from door to door, Margaret would come across many young mothers with babes in arms. Soon enough, she'd come across enough of these mothers to establish a weekly meeting for them, in the name of the church of course. Her first group of mothers came from an area called One Mile Bridge:

> It struck me that these people were in a very out of the way place. There are from twelve to sixteen big families of them, and almost all the mothers have babies. The possibility suggested itself to my mind of getting these mothers together and institute a mothers' meeting. The first mother spoken to about this was a very nice intelligent woman. She seemed delighted. 'I have thought many a time about that,' she said 'and wished some one would come to visit us. But no one ever does come to visit this place.' Then I decided upon forming a meeting next week. The next question to be settled was where to meet. Mrs Coleman's house was suggested as the most convenient in the place.[18]

The mothers' meetings were a great success and in late May Margaret notes in her diary that there were eleven mothers and ten children at the meeting in One Mile Bridge. The group felt quite at home with one another and when the meeting was over they weren't in a hurry to leave. They sat with their babies on their lap, speaking of their experiences or of their health. Margaret had succeeded in creating a bond of friendliness between these strangers.

Soon enough Margaret was arranging mothers' meetings all over the place. By the end of July there were regular meetings at One Mile Bridge, Basin Pocket, South Ipswich and Newtown in the Ipswich area. And the meetings were not only for mothers; meetings were now being arranged for children also. At an evening meeting on 2 September in West Ipswich, over a hundred children were present.

However, all this furious activity, going from one place to another and visiting up to fifteen households a day, started to take its toll on Margaret's health. Two months after starting her work, she caught a cold on her way to One Mile Bridge. Her doctor, Mr Lightoller, tells her that a chill in the blood has caused a partial suspension of her circulation, which in turn has affected the nervous system. Margaret suspends her activities and stays in bed for a fortnight. But it was no wonder that Margaret was frequently catching cold. She would walk everywhere and often mentioned in her diary that the weather had been particularly wet and had flooded roads and made them impassable.

Margaret felt particularly tired in July. One night she was weary and had to address a large gathering of people. She notes:

> There was a fair attendance at Amberley Church in the evening, but I was utterly unfit to conduct the meeting, feeing tired, languid and out of spirits. I could not remember a thing I had prepared to say, being in that state before starting. I took the MS

along with me in case of a failure of memory and had to take to sheer reading after all. I never remember to have felt more miserable. Was it real unbelief and want of faith? God grant it may never happen again.[19]

There is a gap in her diary for August and it seems that she does not visit anyone. By September, it is her sister Mary Anne's health which concerns her. Mary Anne is in hospital, and Margaret arranges that her sister resigns her post at Cribb & Foote so that she can go to the countryside to recuperate.

In the few short months that she had been working for the Central Congregational Church, Margaret had achieved a great deal. She had changed the minds and opinions of many, but she had also seen her own preconceived ideas alter too. One particular resident of Basin Pocket had come in for stern criticism in July, with Margaret noting that: 'many in the south end of the Pocket are regular heathens and the women as hard as flints, quite a different type to any I've seen in Ipswich yet'. But by late September, she had changed her mind, saying: 'I am beginning to change my opinion about Basin Pocket. The woman, who has been most on my mind since my first visit as the hardest, most callous and unimpressionable of any yet seen, was quite different today.'

Margaret's progress is discussed in the church deacons' reports on 26 August. The reports note that Margaret's term of engagement is due to cease in a month, as her six-month trial period is over. It was then agreed that Margaret would continue in post permanently on the same salary. A month's notice from each party would be needed before termination of contract. Margaret had evidently impressed her employers at the church.

There is little further mention of Margaret's work in the deacons' minutes until late November 1889. Then, a note states that a letter has been received from Margaret stating that her health has not been good of late. Margaret suggests that she should be relieved of her work for the time being, or be paid less salary for the work that she able to do, until her health is restored. The meeting decides to advise Margaret to do whatever work that she can and be paid half of her salary for the next three months.

But, less than two months after writing the letter to her employers, Margaret had married. It is unknown whether she continued to work for the Central Congregational Church in Ipswich after her marriage in January 1890. She certainly didn't need to work any more, for financial reasons anyway. She had just married a very wealthy man.

4

James Josey first saw the Australian continent from aboard the convict ship *Eden II*. This was the last convict ship to arrive in the colony of New South Wales, the date being 18 November 1840. James, the son of sawyer Richard Josey and Elizabeth Nicholls, was born on 21 August 1821 in Aldworth, Berkshire, England. The then nineteen-year-old Josey was a passenger on *Eden II* as the result of robbing a wagon, and as this was his second offence, he was sentenced on 22 February 1840 to fifteen years and transportation for his recklessness.

James was quite a lad. According to his own family, he had been a delinquent since his youth. Stories abounded within the family of him appearing before magistrates for robbery on the King's Highway and for living illegally in a hulk on the river Thames. His brother and sister kept themselves out of trouble, but James found himself with a one-way ticket to Australia before he'd entered his second decade.

On his arrival at Port Jackson in Sydney, Australia, it was noted that he was five feet five inches in height. He had sallow eyes, brown hair and a nose which was a little crooked. He possessed two moles underneath his jaw and had tattoos of a woman encircled in a wreath on his upper right arm, a tattoo of the letters JJ, tattoos of a mermaid, an anchor, and the letter J on his lower left arm. It was proved that he could read, but not write. He was single and Protestant.

By April 1841 James was on his way to Moreton Bay in Queensland. He worked on farms in the Limestone area which is 40 km to the west of Brisbane. The area had been established in 1826, when hills of limestone were discovered around the river Bremer. Five convicts were sent to quarry the limestone and a lime-burning kiln was erected. During the next fifteen years the area became a convict colony, and only a few settlers were admitted. But by 1842 the area was opened up for free settlement, and a small town grew there. The town was named Ipswich in 1843.

James Josey worked hard on the farms and kept himself out of trouble. It is possible that he was allowed to ply his trade as a sawyer also. Six years later, on 12 April 1847, he received his ticket of leave (number 47/373), which meant that he was free to do as he wanted as he had completed his punishment. With this ticket he could take up any occupation and soon enough he was running a business with a carpenter named William Vowles. They established a saw mill at Pine Mountains. And with another sawyer called Crouch, the three men became pioneer sawyers in Pine Mountain, and very successful too. Their business cut most of the timber used in building the new town of Ipswich.

Twelve years later, in 1859, James Josey purchased two portions of land from the government in partnership with George Franklin. The two bought over 600 acres in total near Opossum Creek for the price of two Australian dollars an acre. Three years later, Josey had bought his partner's share and from 1868 he began acquiring more land. During the 1870s it was estimated that he was the owner of 2,700 acres, and by 1885 he owned 10,000 acres in the area.

His main home was a property known as Eden Station, built on 420 acres at Redbank Plains. This farm kept cattle and grew timber and, later, sugar and cotton crops. Josey's progress in life and prosperity was considered so remarkable that the governor of Queensland would take visitors to Eden Station to show how convicts could succeed in the new colony. This is how a correspondent from the *Queensland Times* described the Eden Station property and its owner in an article 'A Home in the Bush' on 4 April 1876. It seems that he was very pleased with what he saw:

> Eden Station, the property of Mr James Josey, is situated on Opossum Creek, adjoining Redbank Plains and about twelve miles from Ipswich and sixteen from Brisbane. There is a road leading from Redbank Plains to the homestead, but to a stranger it seems rather an intricate approach to a man's dwelling, who has added so largely to the public purse – more particularly when one comes to the ruins of a tumbled-down bridge on Woogaroo Creek, most of which was carried away by the last floods; but strange to say, no steps have as yet been taken by the Government to make it passable.
>
> This, of course, is not the Eden where mother Eve, like the rest of her sex, bamboozled poor old Adam; but it certainly deserves the name; and were such men as Goldsmith, Cowper or Campbell existing in Queensland, what simple food for their literary genius could they find among the lonely recesses of this romantic place?
>
> This beautiful homestead, which is a model of perfection, is the reward of energy and persevering toil, and Mr Josey may be proud of what he has done. Though many years have been spent improving and forming such a residence, yet it is pleasant to know that he has succeeded in reducing the wild forest to a state of such excellent order. The dwelling itself is a beautiful two-storied building, 60 feet by 30 feet, and divided up into twenty-six apartments, with verandas and balconies all round. The site of the house commands a most picturesque view of the surrounding country, as far as the watershed which separates the waters of the Oxley and Opossum Creeks and thence to Mount Flinders. The natural scenery of the place is magnificent, and that

which crowns the whole is a fine lagoon in front of the building, from the edge of which the land rises gently to the summit of the mountain.

The property at Eden consists of 6,000 acres, 1,000 of which was purchased from the New South Wales Government, and the other 5,000 is leased land, the conditions on which Mr Josey has fulfilled, and obtained the certificates. The timber on this property is of the best quality, and will become very valuable in the future. The land is also very rich in iron-stone, and coal crops out in various parts of the run. Mr Josey was fortunate in securing about 500 acres at Redbank Plains, where cotton, sugar, etc. have been most successfully grown, and as the land is of an excellent quality, he can readily let it, at a good rent, to tenants who prefer to gain a little experience, and obtain a good stock of tools and team of bullocks – which Mr Josey never fails to give his outgoing tenants on the most reasonable terms – before starting out for themselves.

Mr Josey has added largely to nature by the formation of an excellent garden and orchard, both of which are well stocked with the best selections of various trees and shrubs which make up a well-arranged garden and orchard. The orange-trees and grape-vines are looking remarkably well, and their healthy appearance gives proof of the care bestowed upon them by the attentive and willing hands of their owner. All the leased and purchased land is divided and sub-divided into paddocks for breeding mares (of which Mr Josey has many), cattle, sheep etc. The horses and cattle, notwithstanding the long drought, are doing very well, and up to the present show no signs of suffering from want of grass or water.[20]

Eden Station was a family home and James Josey very much the family man. He married a few days before Christmas 1849. His bride was Harriet Catherine Harris, who had been born in Stepney, London, in May 1833. She was the daughter of John Faint Harris and Harriet Catherine Stamford Hough. She had also travelled with her parents on the ship *Eden II* in November 1840, suggesting that a member of her family too was a convict. They were married at St John's Church, Ipswich on 22 December 1849. James Josey was 28 years old and his bride had just turned

16 years. The couple were married under license rather than by banns, because Harriet was under the age of consent. They also had to secure the permission of her father, John Harris, and the permission of the authorities[21] also, as James Josey was still technically a convict at the time (his full sentence would terminate in 1855). Seventeen children were born to the couple, with thirteen of them surviving to adulthood: Harriet, born 16 July 1851; Richard, born 25 March 1853 but died as a child; Emma, born 5 January 1855; Elizabeth, born 4 October 1856; the twins Adam and Eve, born 4 September 1858 (Adam died at four years old); James, born 7 September 1860; Benjamin George, born 10 July 1862; Ann Mary, born 22 November 1863 but died six weeks later; Alfred William, born 29 January 1865; Thursa Ellen, born 30 September 1866; Kate, born 31 January 1868 but who died as a child; Mahala, born 7 April 1869; Naomi, born 26 June 1870; John North, born 28 September 1871; Andrew, born 13 November 1872 and finally Ruth Jessie, born 7 July 1875. Their mother Harriet died at 56 years old on 15 January 1889.

5

Some of James Josey's children were still quite young when their mother died; the youngest, Ruth Mary was thirteen years old. Perhaps Margaret had called on the family at Eden Station after the death of the mother. But there was much amiss in the Josey household after the death of Harriet. It is believed that many of the children were estranged from their father and would have little to do with him. He had apparently tried to keep stories of his youthful indiscretions from the family. But there were also reports within the family that James had become very religious (and perhaps this was as a result of meeting Margaret). James also believed that there was much a 'mother' could do for his children, despite the fact that many of them were adults by now. And

James too needed some company in his old age. He found this companionship in the guise of Margaret Jones from the Central Congregational Church, Ipswich.

One wonders what Margaret got out of this sudden relationship? She was aware that her position with the church was not guaranteed for ever, in spite the warm words of the deacons in the past few months. And even if it had been a job for life, Margaret couldn't guarantee that her health would continue to be well enough to travel around daily, in all weathers, for ever. She would be celebrating her forty-eighth birthday soon; her health had worried her recently; the work, although enjoyable, was quite challenging too. It wasn't work for an older woman. Margaret needed security in her life. Returning home to Wales to find that stability was not an option. James Josey was recently widowed and he still had some children living at home; he could offer Margaret financial security and she would enjoy the challenge of converting him into a conscientious Christian. It was a situation where everyone could benefit.

It's certain that Margaret must have left quite an impression on James, with all those stories she told of her time in the Middle East, Africa and the United States. Guests around the dinner table at Eden Station must have marvelled at James's new friend. Perhaps he had been bewitched by all that Margaret had achieved. Yes, she would be a good companion for him.

James and Margaret were married as soon as it was diplomatically prudent, a year and a day after the death of his first wife, Harriet. They were married at Margaret's home in Warwick Road, Ipswich, by the Rev. Joseph Walker, the minister at the Central Congregational Church, Ipswich. The witnesses to the marriage were Mary Anne, her half-sister and a gentleman called George Clealand Holliday. It's rather surprising that they were not married in the church; there had been floods in the building a few years earlier and perhaps the church had not been repaired in time.

After the marriage, the newlyweds did not return to the grand house and beautiful estate of Eden Station. The house was far too large for the ageing couple; after all James was now 69 years of age and Margaret was approaching her half century. It was decided that James and Margaret would move into a home on the estate, a house called Langley in the village of Redbank Plains. James had built the house for his son Alfred William on his marriage to Edith Austin. Now, Alfred and his wife and children would move into Eden Station, and James and Margaret would settle in Langley.[22]

Little is known of family life at Langley in the subsequent twelve years, before the death of Margaret in 1902, and that of her husband a few months later. Margaret remained very close to her half-sister Mary Anne and James tried to persuade her husband, William Parry, to invest in a cotton business with him. They were all close to one another and William Parry was one of the witnesses to the death of James in 1903.

6

Mary Anne Jones was a brave eighteen-year-old woman when she set sail from London on the ship *Duke of Sutherland* bound for the other side of the world. The Welshman who would become her husband three and a half years later, William Parry, had already established himself in Australia.

William Parry was born on 23 February 1864, a son to quarryman Owen Parry and his wife Mary of Glan-y-gors, Penmorfa, Tremadog, north Wales. He was one of six children and, as a seventeen-year-old man, he was working as a draper's assistant at Miss Brymer's Draper Shop in High Street, Ffestiniog. Ffestiniog was a slate quarrying village and whilst Lewis Thomas, the 'Coal King' of Blackstone was recruiting slate quarrymen and coal miners eager to join him in Australia, he was also recruiting men with specific skills for businesses in Queensland. It appears that William Parry would have been offered work as a draper in Australia before he left Wales.

Twenty-one-year-old William Parry sailed on the ship *Quetta* out of London docks on 22 September 1885. Before long he was employed as a draper at London Stores, the largest general store in Ipswich, which would become known as Cribb & Foote years later. Amongst the store's customers were German-speaking farmers. William Parry volunteered to learn to speak German in order to assist these farmers with their purchases. William stayed with the firm until he built his own general store and post office, Parry's Corner, in Silkstone.

Mary Anne Jones and William Parry met in November 1888 when Mary Anne also started working at Cribb & Foote. And, as both were Welsh speakers, they also met at Welsh activities held locally. William was the secretary of the Christmas eisteddfod held at Blackstone Welsh Church in 1888 and Mary Anne won the contralto competition that year.[23] Some two and a half years later William and Mary Anne were married and five children were born to the couple. Both were very involved in Welsh community events. Mary Anne and the family would hold fetes, garden parties and concerts outside Parry's Corner shop to raise money for the Comfort Fund, Band of Hope, United Welsh Church Guild etc. The large grounds and fig trees which grew around the shop provided the perfect venue for open-air events in the heat of Queensland. William continued his association with the Blackstone Male Voice Choir, one of the choirs which joined together to form the Blackstone-Ipswich Cambrian Choir.

7

Margaret died at the age of sixty on 18 October 1902. Her health had worried her a great deal throughout her life, and the last six months were particularly difficult. She was given the best care, and was adamant that the Lord God was looking after her from above. The following obituary appeared in the *Queensland Times* three days after her death:

Death of Mrs James Josey

At Redbank Plains, on Saturday last (writes a correspondent), Mrs Josey, wife of Mr James Josey (one of the oldest residents of the district), passed away. The deceased, who was 60 years of age, had been ailing for some time past, and her demise was due to an internal complaint. During her illness she was assiduously attended by Mesdames Dan. and Jas. Jones, and Mrs Hudson (daughters of Mr Josey), Mrs Campbell, and others. Mrs Josey was the eldest daughter of Mr Owen Jones, bookseller, of Rhosllanerchrugog, North Wales. She was born in March, 1842. At the age of 14 she went as a nurse-girl to Birmingham to the Rev. E. B. Frankel (a converted Jew), where she stayed about two years. About this period Mr Frankel and family went to Paris, where they lived for about two years, to which place she accompanied the family. While at Paris, the deceased commenced to study, but, owing to having had only three weeks' schooling previous to leaving home, of course, the task was a very difficult one, but by perseverance she succeeded very well. From Paris they proceeded to Jerusalem, arriving there in the beginning of 1865. There she stayed for about four years, during which time she explored Jerusalem and its historic surroundings, describing her travels in detailed letters to her parents. These letters were eventually compiled in a book entitled 'Palestine, and what I saw there'. From Palestine, she was conveyed to Beyrout, a distance of nearly 150 miles, on a bed, owing to a diseased knee, having been in the hospital for some time previously. At Beyrout, she was kindly received by a lady missionary named Mrs Thompson. After staying there some considerable time she was brought on a water bed to Liverpool, and there treated by the eminent physician, Dr

Thomas. After her recovery she decided to lecture on Palestine throughout Wales and the principal English cities, where she was known as the 'Gymraes o Ganaan'. The lecturing tour resulted in enabling her to send a very substantial sum to the mission work at Beyrout. After spending a few years at home she went as a missionary to Mogador, Morocco, Africa. Being familiar with the French and Arabic languages, she taught in schools there for about four years. Returning to Wales she again lectured on her experiences in Morocco, and published a book on Morocco. Her books found a good sale, seven editions of some thousands being issued. She subsequently decided to go to America, where she lectured in the principal cities, remaining there about two years. Then she returned again to Wales, and having had a few years rest came to Australia arriving in Ipswich in 1889. Here she was appointed town missionary for the Congregational Church. In 1890 she was married to Mr James Josey, of Redbank Plains. During her life she was closely connected with Church work, and took a great interest in teaching the young. The funeral took place on Sunday and was well attended. Mr R. H. Lewis conducted a short and impressive service at the house, whilst the Rev. P. Robertson officiated at the cemetery. In accordance with the wish of the deceased two of her favourite Welsh hymns were sung at the graveside, and their rendition was very touching.[24]

It is evident from this obituary that Margaret had thought carefully about the information that she wanted recorded in a newspaper obituary. She was aware that the end was quite close, and ensured that all the facts were accurate and in the possession of the people best placed to look after her legacy once her flame had been extinguished.

In December 1902, a Welsh-language obituary appeared in newspapers in Wales. Clwydwenfro (John Lloyd James, 1835–1919), a minister with the Congregational Church and a historian, was responsible for the obituary that appeared in *Baner ac Amserau Cymru* and *Y Tyst* on 10 December 1902 and in *Y Cymro* [The Welshman] a day later. Clwydwenfro mentions in the obituary that Margaret had sent him her life story written in her own hand with two photographs, shortly before her death. He remarked that her life story was adventurous and well worth publishing if he received sufficient support. He reflected that many in Wales and the United States remembered her well, and admired her a great deal.[25]

8

James Josey died four months after his wife Margaret, on 21 February 1903, at 81 years of age. Yet, his obituary appeared twice, five years apart, in the newspapers, in the *Queensland Times* firstly, on 24 February 1903:

> It is our sorrowful duty to chronicle the death of Mr James Josey, of Redbank Plains. The sad event occurred at his residence early on Saturday afternoon last. His demise was scarcely unexpected, as he had been gradually failing ever since the death of his wife some four or five months ago. The deceased had attained the ripe age of 82 years, and for upwards of 60 years he had been a resident of the district. He was a native of Reading, Berkshire, England, where he was born on the 1st of August 1821. He came to Australia in 1840, landing at Port Jackson. In the following April he came on to Moreton Bay, and from that year up to the time of his death he resided, as stated, in this district. For the greater part of this time he engaged in pastoral pursuits. Eight daughters and five sons – all of whom are married – are left to mourn the demise of their father. The daughters are Mrs Whitmore Logan (Forest Hill), Mrs George Logan (Colinton), Mrs Dan Jones (Brisbane), Mrs James Jones (Goodna), Mrs Hudson (Redbank Plains), Mrs Alfred Hillier (Goodna), Mrs Joseph Griffith (Rosevale) and Mrs H. Scarr (Brisbane); and the sons are Messers. James Josey (Colinton), Ben Josey (Townsville), John Josey (Kilkivan), Andrew Josey (Goodna) and Alfred Josey (Redbank Plains). The funeral took place yesterday afternoon, the body being interred in the Ipswich cemetery. Dr W. C. Pritchard, rector of St Paul's Anglican Church, impressively conducted the service at the graveside.

Then a second obituary appeared in *The Queenslander* on 28 February 1908:

> On Sunday occurred the death of Mr. James Josey, of Possum Creek, Redbank Plains, at the age of 19 [91], the deceased gentleman almost at once took up pastoral pursuits, and after being engaged for some time on what was then known as the Booval station, he started on his own account in the Redbank district, where ever since he has resided and been engaged in developing that district. For many years he was favourably known as a successful dairy farmer and horse breeder, and he also started the first timber-getting industry in the same locality, the timber used in the flooring and ceiling of the existing premises of Messrs. Cribb and Foote coming from the estate. The deceased was bluff in his manner, but thoroughly respected as one of the pioneers of the district, and for many years was a member of the Purga Divisional Board, in the affairs of which he took a keen and intelligent interest. At the time of his death, Mr. Josey was the owner of 350 acres of the best farming land at Redbank Plains, and of 7000 acres at Possum Creek. He had been married twice, and his second wife predeceased him by four months only... It is understood that the deceased's descendants number some eighty souls.

It is unclear why this obituary appeared in *The Queenslander* some five years after his death.

Following the death of James Josey, his land and possessions were transferred to his trustee, Thomas Cribb, and then in 1907 to James and Alice Cribb. The land was sold in 1912 to a John Fenwick of New South Wales. But by 1937 Moreton Shire Council had acquired the land for arrears in rates. The land was subsequently sold several times and used for logging until 1991. Today Springfield Land Corporation owns the land but James Josey's legacy is still to be seen, although the home Eden Station no longer stands. A new city called Springfield has been built on the Eden Station estate. Several roads in the area have been named after people and places which were important to

James Josey. There is an 'Aldworth Place' in Springfield, named after the birthplace of James Josey in Berkshire, England; an 'Eden Crescent' in Springfield Lakes, named after the homestead and the ship on which James and Harriet travelled to Australia; 'Ellen Circuit', 'Eve Court' and 'Jessie Street' in Springfield Lakes are named after three of Josey's daughters. And James Josey has his own 'Avenue' in Springfield Lakes.[26]

But there is no road named after Margaret, the Welsh lady from Canaan, which is a shame. And it is obvious that her friend Clwydwenfro didn't get enough support to publish Margaret's life story, as she wished, soon after her death in 1902. Having looked carefully through Clwydwenfro's personal papers in the National Library of Wales, I failed to find the notes of Margaret's life in her own handwriting, nor the two photographs she sent him a short time before her death. It's obvious that the twentieth century chose to ignore the story of the adventurous lady from Rhos…

Notes

Part I: Rhosllannerchrugog, north Wales

1   National Library of Wales: Map of Rhosllannerchrugog by John Platt, 1895.

2   H R Vaughan Johnson, *Reports of the Commissioners of Inquiry into the State of Education in Wales Part III* (London, 1847), p.75.

3   Ibid.

4   Ibid.

5   Ibid., pp.75–6.

6   Ibid., p.76.

7   Ibid.

8   J Rhosydd Willimas, *Hanes Rhosllannerchrugog* (Rhosllannerchrugog, 1945), pp.11–12.

9   William Phillips, *Rhos-llannerch-rugog: Atgofion* (Caernarfon, 1955), p.6.

10 *Reports of the Commissioners of Inquiry into the State of Education in Wales Part III*, p.76.

11 *Hanes Rhosllannerchrugog*, pp.21–2.

12 *Reports of the Commissioners of Inquiry into the State of Education in Wales Part III*, pp.76–7.

13 Ibid., p.76.

14 Ibid., p.77.

15 *Hanes Rhosllannerchrugog*, p.22.

16 Meic Stephens (ed.), *The New Companion to the Literature of Wales* (Cardiff, 1998), p.809.

17 Huw Owen, *Capeli Cymru* (Tal-y-bont, 2005), p.156.

18 As an apprentice carpenter, Caradog Roberts made the organ stool which is still used by the organists at Bethlehem to this day.

19   Margaret's birth certificate has not been located. Her birth in
      March 1842 was recorded in her obituary in the *Queensland
      Times* at the time of her death in October 1902.

Part II: From Bethlehem to Jerusalem

1   *Jewish Intelligence* (1865), p.263.
2   Proselytized is to convert/turn from one faith to another.
      'Returning' is the term used when a Jew turns to become a
      Christian.
3   Elias Frankel would not see any of his family again until his
      younger brother Georg visited Jerusalem in 1867.
4   *Jewish Intelligence* (1863), p.21.
5   John Davies et al., *Gwyddoniadur Cymru* (Cardiff, 2008), p.477.
6   Ibid., pp.778–9.
7   Ibid., p.157.
8   *New Welsh Review*, 38 (1997), p.41. A later version of this article
      appeared in *A Tolerant Nation?*, eds. Charlotte Williams, Neil
      Evans and Paul O'Leary (Cardiff, 2003).
9   Ibid., p.42.
10   Frankel retired after nineteen years of service for the London
      Jews Society in 1881, later becoming a village rector, *Jewish
      Intelligence* (1881), p.309.
11   William Thomas Gidney, *The History of the London Society for
      Promoting Christianity Amongst the Jews: From 1809 to 1908*
      (London, 1908), pp.9–30.
12   Ibid., p.34.
13   The print works published a translation of the New Testament
      in Hebrew and an edition of the Van der Hooght Bible, before
      closing its doors in 1818.
14   *The History of the London Society for Promoting Christianity
      Amongst the Jews: From 1809 to 1908*, p.42.
15   Ibid., p.97.
16   *Jewish Intelligence* (1863), p.210.
17   *Annual Report of the LJS* (London, 1865), p.67.
18   Canaan: modern-day Syria, Lebanon and Israel.
19   Roberto Copello, *Jerusalem* (Vercelli, Italy, 2008), p.9.

[20] *The History of the London Society for Promoting Christianity Amongst the Jews: From 1809 to 1908*, pp.101–5.

[21] Kelvin Crombie, *For the Love of Zion: Christian Witness and the Restoration of Israel* (Bristol, 2008), p.51.

[22] Ibid., pp.81–2.

[23] Ibid., p.82.

Part III: The Letters of the Welsh Lady from Canaan

[1] The ship makes its way towards the coast of mainland Italy through the Strait of Bonifacio, which lies between the French island of Corsica and the Italian island of Sardinia. Margaret learns that the first French Emperor, Napoléon Bonaparte (1769–1821) was born at Ajaccio on Corsica.

[2] Margaret was also shown the home of the Italian military and political leader Giuseppe Garibaldi (1807–82) on the island of Caprera, on the north coast of Sardinia.

[3] Vittorio Emanuele II.

[4] 2 Peter 2:22.

[5] The *Godavery* was a 1,423 ton French steamship, built in 1863 by L Arman, Bordeaux for Messageries Maritimes, Marseilles for Indian Ocean and Dutch East Indies services which also made calls at Mediterranean ports. She had clipper bows, one funnel and three masts (rigged for sails). There was passenger accommodation for 28 in 1st class, 41 in 2nd class and 22 in 3rd class and also accommodation for troops. In 1869 she was one of the first ships to transit the newly-opened Suez Canal. The *Godavery* was scrapped in 1898.

[6] Joppa is now known as Jaffa. Joppa was once one of the great ports of the Mediterranean Sea. It became a major gateway for boatloads of arriving immigrants and pilgrims. It is one of the oldest known harbours in the world and mentioned in 2 Chronicles 2:16.

[7] Jonah 1:3.

[8] Ramle is known today as Ramla. Prior to the arrival of the Crusaders in the eleventh century, Ramla was Palestine's capital and it maintained its importance in the Middle Ages as the first stop for the Jerusalem-bound pilgrims who came ashore at Joppa.

9 Matthew 27:57–60.

10 This is in fact incorrect. The ark rested at Ciriath-jearim for twenty years, 1 Samuel 7:2.

11 Adolph Saphira (d. 1891) was a Protestant minister and a Biblical interpreter.

12 Prince Arthur was the third son of Queen Victoria and was born in 1850.

13 Luke 5:18–19.

14 Aaron was a priest and the brother of Moses. Psalm 133:2 describes his beard.

15 Isaiah 53:7.

16 Matthew 27:51.

17 The *ague* is also known as pyrexia which is a fever causing heat in the blood.

18 A local photographer.

19 1 Kings 17:4.

20 Genesis 35:19–20.

21 1 Kings 1:33–4.

22 Joel 1:15.

23 Luke 19:41.

24 She notices men sitting in rows, staring into space smoking their boiling bottles of water (the *sheesha* in Arabic and the *nargileh* in Hebrew).

25 John 11.

26 Robert Thomas (1809–90) won a chair for writing the winning ode at the Chester National Eisteddfod in 1866. For further details, see Part I.

27 Psalm 97:2.

28 Robert Jermain Thomas (1840–66), son of the Rev. Robert Thomas, Hanover Chapel near Abergavenny. He was regarded as the first Protestant missionary to Korea but was killed there in 1866.

29 Genesis 19:15–29.

30 Samuel Gobat (1799–1879). He was the Bishop of Jerusalem from 1846 until his death.

31 Matthew 19:29.

32 By the time that this letter was published on 18 January 1868 in *Y Tyst Cymreig*, Thomas was in his grave, having died on the 6 December 1867 from typhoid fever and congestion of the lungs. The eighteen year-old was a coal miner.

33 This walking stick survives to this day. There is a photograph of it in the photograph section.

34 John Phillips (1810–67) was the first headmaster of Normal College, Bangor.

35 Sukkot.

36 This letter could have come from the 18 January 1868 edition of *Y Tyst Cymreig*.

37 Elizabeth Maria Bowen-Thompson (1812 or 1813–69). For further details, see Part IV, pp.128–9.

Part IV: The Length and Breadth of Wales

1 In her book *Morocco, a'r hyn a welais yno* (Wrexham, 1883), p.35, Margaret complains that her master did not offer to pay her fare home from Beirut to Liverpool. She says that strangers paid for the journey.

2 Dr H O Thomas was a bone specialist from Anglesey. He held surgeries at 11 Nelson Street, Liverpool every Sunday and would often see up to two hundred patients, often without being paid (Mai Williams, *Nene*, May 1985).

3 Gwilym Hiraethog's letter was published on 8, 15, 22 and 29 January 1869.

4 *Y Tyst Cymreig*, 22/1/1869, p.5.

5 Ibid., 29/1/1869, p.6.

6 Mark Twain, *The Innocents Abroad* (New York, 1869), p.xxiv.

7 *Y Tyst Cymreig*, 12/3/1869, p.6.

8 According to the *Queensland Times* on 21 October 1902, there were 'several thousand' copies of the book in one print run.

9 E Wyn James and Bill Jones (eds), *Michael D Jones a'i Wladfa Gymreig* (Llanrwst, 2009).

10 Lewis Jones, *Hanes y Wladva Gymraeg* (Aberdare, 1898), p.31.

11 D G Jones, *Cofiant Cranogwen* (Caernarfon, 1932), p.82.

12 R Tudur Jones, *Grym y Gair a Fflam y Ffydd* (Bangor, 1998), p.184.

13 *The New Companion to the Literature of Wales*, p.427.

14 R Tudur Jones, *Hanes Annibynwyr Cymru* (Swansea, 1966), p.196. Others, however, would disagree that he was the first to deliver the popular lecture. Names mentioned as popular lecturers before the time of Gwilym Hiraethog are Eta Delta, Pugh from Mostyn and Samuel Roberts ('S.R.') and his brother, John ('J.R.').

15 *The New Companion to the Literature of Wales*, pp.623–4.

16 T J Morgan, *Diwylliant Gwerin ac Ysgrifau Eraill* (Llandysul, 1972), p.66.

17 Gerallt Jones, *Cranogwen: Portread Newydd* (Llandysul, 1981), p.48.

18 *Cofiant Cranogwen*, p.88.

19 Ibid., p.89.

20 This advertisement would appear in *Y Tyst Cymreig* until early October 1870.

21 Welsh Biography Online, National Library of Wales: *yba.llgc.org.uk/cy/c3-THOM-JOH-1838.html*

22 *Y Tyst Cymreig*, 15/7/1870, pp.6–7.

23 One of the schools that Elizabeth Bowen-Thompson established survives to this day. The Lebanese Evangelical School for Boys and Girls was founded in 1867 and is located in the village of Ain Zhalta, Chouf, Lebanon. The school was rebuilt after the 1975–90 civil war and reopened in 1998.

24 Nadim Shehad, Oxford Dictionary of National Biography Online: www.oxforddnb.com

25 *Y Tyst Cymreig*, 2/9/1870, p.7.

26 Ibid., 30/9/1870, p.6.

27 Ibid., 7/10/1870, p.7.

28 Ibid., 28/10/1870, p.12.

29 Ibid., 4/11/1870, p.5.

30 Ibid., 25/11/1870, p.7.

31 Ibid., 9/12/1870, p.5.

32 Ibid., 23/12/1870, p.7

33 *Y Tyst a'r Dydd*, 20/1/1871, p.13.

34 Ibid., 24/2/1871, p.11.

35   Ibid., 17/3/1871, p.11.

36   Ibid., 4/8/1871, p.7.

37   Ibid., 26/1/1872, p.2.

38   Ibid., 2/2/1872, p.6.

39   Ibid., 9/2/1872, p.5.

40   *Baner ac Amserau Cymru*, 28/2/1872, p.9.

41   *Y Tyst a'r Dydd*, 8/3/1872, p.7.

42   Ibid., 26/4/1872, p.7.

Part V: Africa and America

1   Margaret Jones, *Morocco, a'r hyn a welais yno*, p.34.

2   *The History of the London Society for Promoting Christianity Amongst the Jews: From 1809 to 1908*, p.488.

3   Ibid., p.489.

4   *Morocco, a'r hyn a welais yno*, pp.104–5.

5   Ira D Sankey (1840–1908) was an American evangelist who travelled the world preaching the gospel.

6   *Morocco, a'r hyn a welais yno*, pp.105–115.

7   NLW Ms 9263A.

8   *Y Tyst a'r Dydd*, 9/3/1883, p.13.

9   *Y Cronicl*, June 1883, p.185.

10   *Y Tyst a'r Dydd*, 2/2/1883, p.12.

11   *Baner ac Amserau Cymru*, 28/3/1883, p.11.

12   *Y Tyst a'r Dydd*, 19/1/1883, p.15.

13   *www.norwayheritage.com/p_ship.asp?sh=bothn*

14   *Baner ac Amserau Cymru*, 20/6/1883, p.10.

15   *Wrexham Advertiser*, 9/6/1883, p.6.

16   *Y Genedl Gymreig*, 10/10/1883, p.7.

17   Hywel Williams, *Cassell's Chronology of World History* (London, 2005), p.437.

18   *Y Tyst a'r Dydd*, 5/6/1885, p.10.

19   Ibid., 17/7/1885, p.11.

Part VI: Australia

1   *Australian Dictionary of Biography*, pp. 260–1.

2   The government of Queensland would pay for the journey to Australia of some particular categories of immigrants and their families, depending on the type of people required at the time: female domestic servants or married couples without children, for example. Applicants were required to pay the sum of £1 and another £1 for each member of the family. To be eligible, they would have to be unable to pay their own passage, and would not have resided previously in any Australian colony. They then had to live in Queensland permanently.

3   Assisted/nominated/remittance passengers: It was possible for any person born or living in Queensland to secure a passage to the colony for a friend or relative who lived in Europe. Payment was required for the passage warrant. The warrant was then forwarded to the friend or relative in Europe. Then a representative of the Queensland government would organise the voyage for the immigrant.

4   *Ipswich Congregational Church: Jubilee 1853–1903* (Ipswich, 1903), p.25.

5   'Miss Jones' Lady Visitors Diary of Work', p.4. This is held at John Oxley Library, Queensland State Library, Brisbane.

6   Ibid., p.138.

7   Ibid., p.65.

8   Ibid., pp.92–3.

9   Ibid., pp.73–4.

10   Ibid., pp.21–2.

11   Ibid., pp.46–8.

12   Ibid., pp.93–4.

13   Ibid., p.62.

14   Ibid., p.17.

15   Ibid., p.8.

16   Ibid., p.130.

17   Ibid., pp.107–8.

18   Ibid., pp.26–7.

19   Ibid., pp.101–2.

20   *Queensland Times*, 4/4/1876, p.4.

21   He was given permission to marry by the governor of New South Wales. New South Wales Convict Records 4/4514 Folio 161, State Records Authority of New South Wales, Kingswood, NSW.

22   Langley is 83, Johnston Street, Redbank Plains today.

23   Mary Anne Parry continued to sing and compete throughout her life and, at the age of 70, she won the veteran's solo at the Queensland Eisteddfod.

24   *Queensland Times*, 21/10/1902.

25   *Y Tyst*, 10/12/1902, p.13.

26   'Pioneer Place Names', Ipswich City Council Planning Branch.

Index

Also by Eirian Jones:

Enclosure riots on a lonely Welsh hillside

The WAR
of the Little
ENGLISHMAN

Eirian Jones

y Lolfa

£6.95

The Welsh Lady from Canaan is just one of
a whole range of publications from Y Lolfa.
For a full list of books currently in print, send
now for your free copy of our new full-colour
catalogue. Or simply surf into our website

www.ylolfa.com

for secure on-line ordering.

TALYBONT CEREDIGION CYMRU SY24 5HE
e-mail ylolfa@ylolfa.com
website www.ylolfa.com
phone (01970) 832 304
fax 832 782